ㄣ

PATG1094290-B

BASIC BOOKS IN EDUCATION

Editor: *Kathleen O'Connor, B.Sc., Principal Lecturer in Education, Rolle College, Exmouth*
Advisory Editor: *D. J. O'Connor, M.A., Ph.D., Professor of Philosophy, University of Exeter.*

Schooling in the Middle Years
Music

Music has often been regarded as separate from the rest of the curriculum, of limited appeal and to be taken seriously only with a small minority of children. Miss Glynne-Jones shows how musical awareness can be stimulated among all children in a class or school by the adoption of an approach very different from the traditional music or 'singing' lessons. Musically, as with other aspects of development, children proceed at differing rates according to their abilities and opportunities. Thus the middle school teacher will find children of eight and nine years at differing stages of musical understanding. In each chapter, therefore, fundamental activities are considered so that the reader may appreciate the continuous sequence of musical development.

Although much has been done in other areas of the curriculum, little consideration has hitherto been given to re-examining music in the light of current knowledge of child development. As Miss Glynne-Jones demonstrates, it is only now that the true musical potential of children is beginning to be discovered.

At the end of each chapter there is a summary and further reading list, and the book contains a full bibliography, glossary and index.

Schooling in the Middle Years

Music

M. L. GLYNNE-JONES L.R.A.M. A.R.C.M.

SENIOR LECTURER IN MUSIC
TRENT PARK COLLEGE OF EDUCATION

LINNET BOOKS

First published 1974

Published by
MACMILLAN EDUCATION LIMITED
London and Basingstoke

*Associated companies and representatives
throughout the world*

Printed in Great Britain by
ROBERT MACLEHOSE AND CO LTD
The University Press, Glasgow

ISBN: 0-333-12253-4

Contents

Foreword

Until recently, the teaching of music in most primary schools did not keep pace with developments in other aspects of learning. Now, many children have opportunities to make their own music, individually, in groups of their own choosing, or in a planned workshop situation.

This book shows how pupils in the middle years, working with a teacher who understands the growth and development of children and who is also a good musician, can become aurally sensitive and, as their understanding and intellectual grasp of music increases, are able to shape rhythm, melody and harmony into satisfying forms. They can also comprehend something of the world of music of the past and of today. The book is an account of shared experiences. As it is 'concerned with the potential development in music of all children' so it depicts the demands likely to be made on any teacher working in the ways described with pupils between the ages of eight and thirteen.

November 1970   J. M. SYKES,
                                      Her Majesty's Inspector of Schools,
                                   with special interest in music, 1946–71

1 Early Development

Any discussion on musical education in the middle years must take into account all that has previously happened to children musically. We cannot begin to understand the functioning of eight year olds without knowledge of their development since birth, nor can we presume to teach music to young children without knowing something of their development. Specialist knowledge of the subject matter is not enough. Unfortunately few adults count themselves musically educated; in general, adults support the mystique which has grown up around those who know about music. This attitude is perpetuated by the way in which music is taught in school. Teachers hesitate to interfere in the work of their music specialist colleagues, although in many cases their knowledge of children's development might result in more genuine musical activity in schools than does the musical expertise of the specialist.

In recent years there has been a liberation in children's painting and writing activity, with remarkable work produced by ordinary, not especially gifted children. We now know that if their environment stimulates and feeds children's imaginations, they become writers and painters within their own society. This rarely happens in music, yet very young children respond to sound with intense interest and fascination; a RHYTHMIC quality pervades their activity, and their voices are used to express various moods. The beginnings of musical expression are present for all to see in the activity of young children, but somehow it is put off-course and seldom develops in the same way as other forms of expression. This must inevitably be attributed to the experiences of children in school. It is a matter of deep concern for all involved in education, that most children are deprived of the opportunity to develop musically; this concern is evident in current literature about musical education.

In recent years a similar concern has been felt about children and mathematics, for mathematical education often failed to develop in children a capacity to think mathematically and to operate the laws of mathematics with understanding. At the same time the work of developmental psychologists, and in particular the work of Piaget, has given us insight into children's intellectual development, into the growth of mathematical thinking and the development of language. Our present knowledge of concept formation has resulted in a revolution in the teaching of mathematics, and attention is being directed to other areas of children's learning. It is not logical to assume that the developmental stages in Piagetian theory apply to all children's functioning *except* music, and therefore we must find out if there is a relationship between children's intellectual development and their musical functioning.

When children arrive at nursery or infant school, it is very obvious that musical development has already taken place, and that they have acquired considerable skill in vocalising and in making sounds on an instrument by banging, whether it is a drum, or saucepan, or the side of a chair. Let us look at the development of these dual aspects of musical activity.

The vocal sounds babies make soon cease to be mainly an expression of discomfort and begin to express content in babblings and murmurings. They gradually learn to repeat their own sounds more and more accurately, though a newly discovered sound may be repeated at first with slight variations in PITCH and DYNAMIC, or of the sound itself. As skill develops, the variations occur less frequently and a repertoire of sounds is built up. Once the skill of imitating their own sounds is developed, they begin to imitate sounds made by external sources; this involves vocal accommodations and is a more complex activity. As a result of this imitative behaviour, most young children develop a wide vocal range which is evident in their play. In excitement or content, or in sheer enjoyment, children cannot help using their voices to express their mood. Sounds are also used in play to symbolise things about which they have some understanding.

A boy (3.6) travelled round a classroom being a car; his arms steered an imagined wheel, and his voice made the sound of the engine as the gear was changed.

By the time they are four or five years old, many children have developed a remarkable pitch accuracy in singing tunes they have learned; other four and five year olds have great difficulty in reproducing a pattern of two or three notes, and some may not yet have learned to do this. However, tunes which are accurately sung, cannot always be sung at a pitch begun by someone else: accommodating to a specific pitch is a later development. For this reason young children may seem unable to sing a tune accurately when they are singing with each other at a pitch set by the teacher, though many of them could probably do so at a pitch they set for themselves. The growth of this skill is fostered by the singing activity in good nursery and infant schools. In these schools singing time is very like story time, with the children gathered informally round the teacher, so that they can focus their attention on the song. The singing is unaccompanied and pitched in the developed range of children's voices, for it is only by beginning singing activity in the developed vocal range, that the gradual extension of it is fostered. There is evidence that the vocal range of infant children is lower than has previously been considered, and although the sounds they make as they play are often very high shrieks and yells, the range in which they can sing in tune with someone else (i.e. accommodate to specific patterns of pitch), is likely to be much lower. There is often an opportunity for children to use their voices to make non-singing sounds as part of their work in movement and drama; this helps them to discover what their voices can do, what high or low sounds they can make, and what different sorts of sounds they can make. In these ways children develop a confidence in using their voices and the inhibiting effects of premature formal training are avoided, although no opportunity is missed – as far as is humanly possible – to foster their developing vocal skill.

The development of causing sound on an instrument has its

beginnings in the reflexive kicking of babies, as their limbs come into contact with the surfaces near-by; a dull thud is probably the first sound caused in this way. From this develops the deliberate causing of sound by banging limbs against surfaces. When the skill of grasping develops, earlier modes of behaviour are applied to the objects grasped and they are sucked or banged; the banging action causes sound as objects and surfaces come into contact. Young children need to be presented with objects whose sound properties are considered alongside their shape and colour; they need to be of different sizes and made of different materials. In this way banging becomes the first mode of causing instrumental sound. This skill is fostered in homes in which babies are allowed to bang objects, and nursery and infant schools continue this by creating opportunities for children to use percussion instruments. However, the school environment is a specialist one, and the provision of materials must be made according to children's needs as they develop. The criteria to be taken into account in selecting instruments are discussed in Chapter 9. They naturally apply to infant and first school provision.

It is the materials presented to three and four year olds which cause their behaviour. Their activity is the result of whatever catches their attention, and continues until something else catches their eye. There is no sense of concentration as adults know it, save on the action of the moment, even while the eye is surveying possible new activity. Whatever musical instrument catches the attention is played; perhaps it is important not to have things always in the same place in a classroom, for this reason.

The teacher of a nursery class moved the instrument table from a dark corner of the room to a place opposite the door. She observed that the children used the instruments more often than before, in particular at times which followed entry into the room. She also observed that the arrangement on the table tended to govern children's choice of instrument. Clearly the way she organised the room had an immediate effect on the children's activity and their subsequent development.

This is characteristic of the behaviour of four and five year olds. Their early experience builds up ideas of the sounds made by different instruments and they learn to expect certain results from their actions. The results are often attractive musically, perhaps with a regular BEAT or TIME PATTERN present.

A group of five year old boys decided to make a band. They marched round the classroom playing drums and cymbals rhythmically.

We may be misled into thinking that children of this age, who behave in this way, know exactly what they are doing, and act with definite musical ideas in mind, i.e. to play intentionally a regular beat or time pattern, and to keep in time with each other. But at this time, the intention is usually a general one and concerned with their actions. In the example above, the children's intention was to play instruments and march round the room like a band. However, while they carried out their general intention, they intuitively played their own time patterns and kept in time with each other, as a result of the ideas they had assimilated from all the music they had heard.

The activity of this band of five year olds is characteristic of children's functioning when ideas are intuitively used. There is no mental analysis of the ideas for the view is a global one. During this pre-operational stage of intellectual development, children need to explore and experiment with as wide a selection of musical materials as possible (see Chapter 9), in order to build the foundations of ideas which later will become concrete, specific, and capable of analysis.

A group of students observed the behaviour of a five year old on his visits to a music room. He looked round the room and his attention was caught by a drum. He walked over to it, picked up a beater and began to play. As he played he looked round again, and this time a melodica caught his attention. This behaviour continued for several visits. At first the students thought that his working was entirely random and forgotten, once it was completed, but they had to think again when they realised he was becoming more skilful and his music was becoming progressively more coherent. They observed that he was learning to play in time, and was intuitively repeating patterns and balancing the PHRASE STRUCTURE of his music.

EXAMPLE 1. Music by a five year old boy in which repetition and the balance of PHRASES are used intuitively; the shape of the melody is the result of his perception of the length of the instrument and is bounded by the top and bottom notes. The bottom note was hit very hard because he was very sure of its position.

The skill of playing percussion instruments is usually developed by the time the children reach middle school. If the idea of causing 'a good sound' (TONE) has arisen, the point of aim and the way to hold a beater will be understood. This technique will be applied to the tuned and untuned percussion children use in school. They should also have discovered the difference in sound caused by beaters made of different materials. Although children of seven and eight may be aware of the tone and technique in other people's work, they may not yet have learned to apply the technique to their own playing, and may still be concerned in causing sound in their own way. Drums may be hit on the rim or on the side; they may be placed flat on the floor, or on their side, or strung round the neck to make marching possible. Instruments which are played in ways other than banging may present an initial difficulty.

A boy (6) was mystified that he could blow the melodica and not make a sound. He had watched other children and the teacher playing it, but had not perceived their action of pressing the keys.

When there is adequate working space, it is usual to see children sitting or kneeling on the floor with their instruments spread around them. Some may use more than one instrument, probably too many at first, in attempts at complexity and variety.

The following examples reflect the enormous stride forward in children's thinking which occurs at this time. Their mode of thought becomes less and less intuitive, as they begin to operate with definite ideas in mind which are capable of analysis. One of the first concepts to become established is the idea of PULSE and many early compositions consist only of beats (see Examples 11 and 12).

EXAMPLE 2

TEACHER 'What did she do?'

BOY (6) 'She did separate notes and a slide.'

The pattern of pitch was intentional, though the action was still governed by her perception of the length of the instrument.

Four seven year old boys played drums to the rest of the class. When one of them left the room in the middle of the performance, the others did not notice. Though they were playing at the same time as each other, they were only concerned with their *own* action: their view was egocentric.

A boy (6) used two beaters to play a xylophone; no real coherence emerged in his playing and he often missed the instrument and hit the floor.

BOY (6) 'I was keeping time.'

BOY (6) 'Then you went slower and slower.'

A boy (7) intended to play a regular beat; there were irregularities in his playing which he did not perceive.

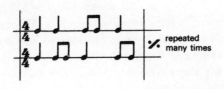

EXAMPLE 3. Two girls (7) played drums, using time patterns intuitively. They knew the *whole* pattern, but did not perceive the constituent parts.

GIRL (7) 'At first they were very loud and then they went soft.'

EXAMPLE 4. They knew about GLISSANDI, keeping in time, and making an ending with a loud bang; the time pattern was intuitively played and perceived as a whole.

The older children in Examples 3 and 4 had chosen to work together. As children's activity becomes less egocentric, and they start to see the world from a viewpoint other than their own, they can begin to co-operate; this has not been intellectually possible before. Children may have chosen to play their music at the same time as each other, but could not co-operate to produce an end result as they had no specific intention other than their action, i.e. actually playing an instrument: their viewpoint was egocentric, and their ideas intuitively used. With the growth of operational thinking it becomes possible to communicate a more specific intention because one now exists, and the genuine exchange of ideas begins to take place. However, this development may not have been fostered in some infant and first schools, and children may not have developed a capacity to communicate their ideas to each other in a working situation in music. In a formal classroom situation there is rarely an opportunity for children to work together and to discuss the problems they encounter, and as this is a skill which like any other has to be learned, it may not have begun to develop. Teachers meeting children in junior or middle schools, need to assess their stages of social development and ability to co-operate, and create opportunities for them to work together if the experience has been lacking. As soon as children *do* choose to work together, problems of organising music emerge: how to end together, how to begin (see Chapter 4). Some eight year olds will be well advanced in their understanding of the basic ideas of musical form, but others may not have perceived this problem at all.

Tunes are at first the result of the action of banging, or blowing, or pressing keys. A development is apparent in the behaviour of the six and seven year old compared to that of the five year old described on page 14. The six and seven year olds look at what they are doing much more, but the notes of the tune may still not be selected for the notes' sake but as a result of their own action, of their perception of the shape (top and bottom) of the instrument, and their own spatial awareness as they move the beater or their fingers.

EXAMPLE 5 Boy (6.6). The MELODIC shape is the result of the action of blowing and sucking; he intended to keep time, using time patterns intuitively.

As the action of banging or blowing becomes more skilful and rhythmic organisation begins to emerge, tunes are shaped by the rhythms used (see the example above). This shaping is not intentional, though to the listener, the tune may seem clearly organised and coherent. The first intentional tunes made up by children often lose the verve and spontaneity characteristic of their earlier work; much more is involved in carrying out a definite idea in effort, concentration, memory, and judgement.

EXAMPLE 6. Girl (7). The playing was slow at first, but as she became more familiar with the feel of playing her pattern, it became faster.

One of the first intentional organisations of pitch which appears is a time pattern played at different pitches, i.e. used as a SEQUENCE (see the example above).

The listening response of seven and eight year olds varies tremendously from day to day, according to their present concentration span or according to the mood of the class; this is affected by a host of factors. It will not be very advanced if children lack experience of listening. Music needs to be part of the environment of nursery and infant schools, not played to children with enforced stillness for 'appreciation', but played to those who choose to listen. Just as the instruments played by young children have caught their eye, so the music to which they listen, needs to have caught their ear. They may listen for a minute, or even less, or they may be able to sustain their concentration for longer.

A teacher of a class of six year olds kept an old record player and a collection of 78 r.p.m. records for children's own use in a screened corner of the room. She also played records frequently in class, for children to listen to, or not, as they chose.

If children are free to enter the world of listening in this way, because their interest is caught, a listening response develops; music invariably invokes a response in young children, whether it is the mood, or the sound of the instruments, or the rhythm or melody which catches their attention. The selection of 'suitable' music is not necessary, for their ears are as open to sounds as their eyes are open to sights. It is only by experiencing different and varied sounds that children can come to perceive, at a later stage in their development, the ideas used in our musical culture.

When children begin to think operationally, i.e. with definite ideas in mind which are capable of analysis, they begin to discuss the music they make up, using their own language to name the ideas; for example the idea of tone is usually referred to as a 'good sound'. At this time the idea of making a written record of music also emerges. Children first represent their music by drawings, indicating their focus on the playing of an instrument and their inability to analyse the musical ideas used. At a later stage words or numbers, or their own notational symbols supported by drawings, are used.

EXAMPLE 7*   Girl (6.6)

first ⬭ 4 taps   then shake the 🥄

And then start doing the Black then I
will use the other Block at the same
time use the 🥄 then start again.

EXAMPLE 8*   Girl (6.10)

▭	4 Fifth
	4 second

▭ 4 first

🔘 4 third

◯ 4 fourth
  4 sixth

EXAMPLE 9*   Boy (7)

* Throughout the text an asterisk denotes notated by the child.

123   1234

12   12   123

EXAMPLE 10*   Boy (7)

In most infant schools part of the room is set aside for musical
activity, with a selection of instruments set out on a trolley or
table. The children should be free to work in their own way
when they wish, the only limitation being to ensure that the room
is quiet during certain periods of the day. Given this experience,
they should have learned in some way to be responsible for their
own work, and their interest and fascination in sound and in the
skill of causing it, should be as alive as it was in their early childhood.

SUMMARY

Young children learn to imitate the vocal sounds they have made
themselves, and later, sounds made by external sources. From this
early experience a wide voice range develops. This is evident in play,
though it does not indicate the range of singing voice, which is often
lower and more restricted. Many four and five year olds can reproduce
tunes accurately at their own pitch, but cannot always sing in tune to a
given pitch. This develops later.

The intuitive use of simple musical ideas develops from early
instrumental (banging) activity, in which tunes result from the action
of banging and perception of an instrument's shape. During the
egocentric stage children play alongside each other; genuine co-
operation develops as they decentre, and as concrete ideas are established. At this time they begin to score their music using drawings,
words and signs. The quality of listening and singing experience, and
of instrumental opportunity during the first school years, bears directly
on the quality of later learning.

FURTHER READING

Bailey, Eunice *Discovering Music with Young Children*
    Methuen, 1958
Brearley, Molly (ed.) *Fundamentals in the First School*
    Blackwell, 1969 (Chapter 7)

2 Rhythm and Time

In any piece of children's music, whether its construction completely lacks intention (pre-operational thinking), or is partly or fully intentional (operational thinking), ideas of time, pitch, and form are evident. In tracing the development of musical concepts it is helpful to deal with these ideas separately, bearing in mind that together they give a unified reflection of children's musical understanding at any one time.

We have seen that concrete ideas of time usually develop earlier than those of pitch, and that the concept of a regular beat is likely to be the first that becomes established. Early examples of children's notation reflect this focus of attention (see Chapter 1). When the concept of pulse begins to be established, children try to keep time in their music, and until they are satisfied with the result, their whole attention is given to this problem.

EXAMPLE 11   Boy (7)
The occasional ACCENTING of beats was not intentional; the underlining marks places at which he was out of time.

EXAMPLE 12*   Boy (8)
His TEMPO was slow – he needed time to produce the notes accurately.

As their perception and understanding of pulse develop, children learn to set a high standard for themselves of playing in time, and begin to perceive the slightest irregularities in other children's playing.

GIRL (9) 'We went wrong, we didn't keep in time.'
PARTNER 'Most of it was in time though.'
BOY 'Doesn't matter so much with those (glockenspiels), because the sound carries over so much because of the vibration.'
Two eight year old boys, each using a drum, tried to play different rhythms at the same time.
BOY (8) 'You couldn't understand very much what the rhythm was – bom bom, bom bom bom bom, bom – they didn't have a beat.'

Once the idea of playing beats has developed, the idea of not playing beats can emerge, and RESTS, much more helpfully called one-beat-silences at first, are used.

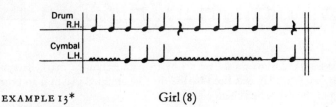

EXAMPLE 13*   Girl (8)

At this stage of their development, children's music reflects a focus on beats, or on beats and rests; time is taken to assimilate their significance fully. During this time louds and softs (dynamics), and different speeds of beat (tempi) begin to be taken into account; drum ROLLS and GRACE NOTES begin to be used in order to make the music more interesting. These ideas will have been assimilated from the listening experience of children which is very likely to include hearing bands of various types, on television if not in the flesh! In this way, the basic concept of regular pulse is used in a musical fashion and dealt with in an increasingly expressive manner.

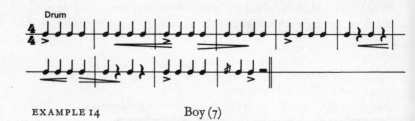

EXAMPLE 14   Boy (7)

EXAMPLE 15. Drum music by a boy (7); underlinings mark irregularities in tempo. He was tired by the time he stopped playing, and the tuning of the drum had changed.

EXAMPLE 16*. Music by the same boy when he was 9; he had found difficulty in learning to play in time. This piece was accurately played.

EXAMPLE 17*   Two boys (9)

This understanding develops at different rates in children, as the examples above illustrate.

In attempts to keep time, counting inevitably becomes involved, as this is an obvious means to children of organising and analysing the music they make up. Teachers have to deal with this idea most carefully to avoid the danger of children counting for its own sake, before its significance in relation to pulse is realised.

A confusion will most probably arise when divisions of the beat are incorporated into the playing.

GIRL (8) 'You know I always play 1 2 3 (tapping ♫ ♩). Well, I thought we'd do something different 1 2 3 4 5 (tapping ♫.♫.♫ ♩).'
The counting was inconsistent even within her own system, and further experience of hearing, playing, and discussing was necessary before she saw that there was a problem. To teach her to copy the teacher's counting by rote would not have helped her to perceive this.

When children have grown beyond the stage of a specific concern for regular beats, the music they make up once more includes the intuitive use of time patterns, as it had done previously. When this occurs, the counting tends to be of the number of notes which are sounded: from the children's point of view this is logical. They need help in drawing the distinction between the number of hits or sounds and the number of beats in the same piece of music, by examples of analysis set by the teacher.

TEACHER 'Play your music again and we'll all keep the beat and count how many beats the music lasts for.'
BOY (8) 'It lasted for thirty-four beats altogether.'
This was accurate!

In this way an awareness grows of the difference between time pattern and pulse, and the inclusion of patterns in the counting of beats. This in turn has to do with notions of whole and part which develop in mathematical thinking at this time. Some children experience great difficulty in assimilating this idea, and there are likely to be great differences of understanding within a class.
Long notes (multiples of the beat) occur initially as a result of the materials chosen, i.e. because the instrument chosen has long-lasting vibrations or is suitable for playing rolls; cymbals, triangles, pianos, autoharps and guitars all produce a long-lasting sound which can be dampened at will. Once notes are used which last for more than one beat, silences of more than one beat begin to be used.

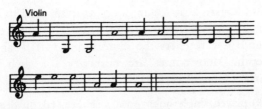

EXAMPLE 18*   Boy (9)

The focal point of this piece of work was the skill of bowing. The BAR
LINES were put in in response to music he had seen, but their significance was not realised; the time patterns were intentional. He referred
to a tuning chart to find out where to write the notes.

See also Example 16.

Children have an intuitive understanding of their own needs as
they develop. Once a concept of a regular beat is established,
however long this has taken, it is very rare for them not to
extend their range of activity by beginning to use instruments in
ways which take them further in their understanding. This is
illustrated in the previous examples in which the new dimension
of long-lasting notes has appeared. Playing long notes deepens
children's absorption in the effects of vibration and they become
curious about the scientific facts of causing sound. Primitive
musical instruments are made by eight and nine year olds at their
own instigation, when they begin to grasp, in a general sense,
the principles involved.

A girl (8) made a zither from balsa wood and elastic bands; she was
not concerned with tuning its strings and used the instrument to strum
time patterns.

Stopwatches are used to time the length of vibration and experiments made to find out the best way of hitting an instrument
(for example a cymbal) to make the vibrations last the longest
possible time.

GIRL (7) 'I can play a much longer note than I used to (on the melodica);
almost for a minute.'

Children learn to assess the length of a note with a stopwatch,
or by counting the number of beats through which it lasts.
It takes time to understand that a two-beat-note lasts until the
beginning of a third beat, or that a five-beat-note lasts until the

beginning of a sixth beat: examples of analysis need to be set by the teacher. These experiences bring the idea of tempo to children's attention and give teachers the opportunity to talk about it in greater depth. Metronomes are necessary for such scientific experiments.

A boy (8) played single notes on a melodica, taking deep breaths so that the notes sounded for as long as possible.

BOY (8) 'He took jolly long breaths!'
TEACHER 'How long did his notes last?'
GIRL (8) 'I didn't get his beat.'
TEACHER 'Could you play it again and tap your beat with your foot, and then we can count.'
BOY (9) 'Let's put the ticker (metronome) on in his time.'

When children begin to demand strict tempo in their own playing, they often ask for the use of a metronome; they can be completely floored by its inflexibility if they have not perceived their own easing of the beat, for example at a CADENCE point. This helps them to perceive the difference between rhythmic and METRIC playing.

If an analysis of the number of beats and sounds in a whole piece of music is made, it can lead to an analysis of the number of sounds on each beat. It is a matter of fine judgement for teachers to decide how far to take this analysis at any one time. The difficulty lies in the possibility of two ways of dividing the beat: into equal parts (♫♫ $\frac{1}{2}\frac{1}{2}$ $\frac{1}{2}\frac{1}{2}$) or into unequal parts (♩♫♫. $\frac{3}{4}\frac{1}{4}$ $\frac{1}{4}\frac{3}{4}$). At first, children often think that the music 'goes faster' if divisions of the beat are present; from their point of view this is logical, as they hear notes sounding in quicker succession to one another. If teachers set an example of keeping the beat by tapping or nodding or counting, children begin to perceive that in fact the beat is not faster although the music sounds quicker to them. Initially, children's global perception of the divisions of a beat is concerned only with the number of sounds, whether they are equal or not; not until this idea is assimilated can they pass on to the next stage of analysis. At a later stage, when efforts are made to analyse the divisions, counting again appears and provides an analytical framework for the idea of equal division of the beat. The contribution of teachers is crucial here, for it sets the example of mathematical analysis from the point of view of the pulse. The following example illustrates this.

A girl (9) played a tune on a xylophone using CROTCHETS and QUAVERS. The teacher asked how the pattern was built and the music was repeated for the purpose of analysis; it *could* be repeated as the composer knew her tune in detail. After a second hearing most of the children in the class perceived that whole and half-beats were being played.

GIRL (9) 'Play some music with thirds (of beats).'

The teacher did so at the piano, keeping a crotchet bass and putting the time pattern over it.

BOY (9) 'Play in sixths (of beats). Play in tenths.'

TEACHER 'I think I shall have to have a slower beat for that. Why?'

BOY 'Because you would have to play terribly fast to get them all in this beat' (demonstrating by tapping on the floor).

This continued for some while, the children counting the number of notes played on each beat, some out loud and some in their head. The teacher then reversed the procedure, asking the children if they could hear the divisions of the beat being played. The language used was mathematical, for these ideas of fractions had already been met by the children in number work. Correct musical terminology, exemplified in the teacher's comments on subsequent occasions was gradually assimilated. Children's *own* use of it emerged later.

The problem of unequal division of the beat is perceived in the same manner; if DOTTED RHYTHMS do not appear in children's compositions, music needs to be played to them which includes such patterns, so that their perception of them can develop. However, given a satisfactory input of music in singing and listening, children usually use these patterns intuitively, so that at an appropriate time their attention can be drawn to them. Dealing with the idea of halves and thirds paves the way for bringing the idea of SIMPLE and COMPOUND TIME to children's notice.

EXAMPLE 19*. Boy (10), practising putting patterns together; he gave no indication on his score of when to end.

EXAMPLE 20*. Two boys, (10), determined to 'conquer' difficult patterning.

In the example on page 29, the teacher joined the children in solving the problem of rhythmic analysis, at the same time presenting models to them of the ideas they were beginning to comprehend. Their attention needed to be drawn to music in our culture using the same devices; music they already knew, as well as unfamiliar works.

TEACHER 'Mozart used this rhythm to open one of his symphonies (playing theme).'
'What songs do you know which use this pattern?'
'The music I played in Assembly had your rhythm in part of it.'

It is mistaken to assume that the initial introduction of an idea at this stage of development can be from the teacher, giving lessons on dotted rhythms or TRIPLETS etc. Certainly, music which includes particular devices needs to be played to children on many occasions, creating opportunities for possible assimilatory activity, but only when the assimilation of an idea is observed by the teacher – this will be when the particular idea is noticed and recognised and used in a piece of music on several occasions – is the time appropriate to bring this to children's notice in discussion.

TEACHER 'Did you notice that rhythm? It was used in . . .'
'Play some music using that rhythm.'
'What time patterns are being used?
'What divisions of the beat did he use?'

Teachers create a situation in which models are presented to children and then have to wait for their perception of the ideas to develop – doing all that is necessary to encourage this – so that a more specific contribution can be made in a meaningful situation, i.e. in the presence (literally the sound) of the idea. What is learnt in this way cannot be forgotten, for it can always be reconstructed: it becomes part of the mental structure of children which is constantly expanded and adapted in the light of new experience. This is a dynamic process in which children are deeply absorbed. Some teachers may fear that if they wait for an appropriate moment to make such a specific contribution, children will not learn very much, if anything at all! However, those teachers who have studied children who have worked in this way, not only in music but in all their school activity, are constantly amazed by the depth and maturity of understanding which develops, and by the way in which problems are perceived and effectively dealt with. These children may certainly not have so many facts learned off by heart – which would probably be forgotten later – but what they do know, becomes part of their permanent understanding.

As we have seen, when children begin to use beats, organising them into a piece of music, the idea of playing some of them extra-loudly emerges; this may be to make a good ending, or to take the audience by surprise in the middle of the music (see Example 14). In this way the idea of accent grows. The following example shows how early notions of accent lead to an awareness of the groupings of beats.

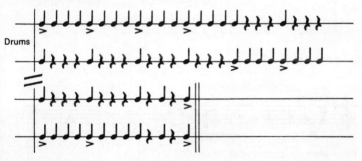

EXAMPLE 21*   Two girls(8)
  GIRL (8) 'She had lots of accents in her music.'
  TEACHER 'Did you notice how she organised her accents?'
  BOY (8) 'Yes, every fourth one.'
In the same lesson four groups of children played music using groupings of four beats. In the weeks following, the class became aware of the frequency with which four-time was used.

TEACHER 'Grouping beats in fours is often called COMMON TIME.'

BOY (9) 'It certainly is common in our class!'

The models of groupings of beats presented to children should not only be two-, three- or four-time, but also include five (two and three, three and two) or seven (three and four, four and three) or seven and eight (in various groupings of two and three), and groupings which change during a piece of music. If their experience *is* limited in the way described, children will be deprived of hearing other, more fluid groupings, and their lack of early assimilatory activity will hinder and sometimes prevent their understanding of these. At a later stage, the spiral of learning returns to the idea of stress and accent when these occur off the beat, and this should lead to an understanding of SYNCOPATION and CROSS-RHYTHM, and devices such as TIED NOTES (see Examples 22, 23) and AUGMENTATION and DIMINUTION (see Example 41).

EXAMPLE 22*   Girls (11)

EXAMPLE 23*   Girls (11)

As these ideas become firmly established, they are used with increasing expressiveness in children's compositions; increasing mobility in musical thinking allows for greater variety and inter-play of ideas; very often new elements appear in their work as a direct result of music heard recently. In all their compositions and improvisations new elements appear, used intuitively at first, among ideas which are used intentionally; reaching out for new things enriches the store of what is already known and operational. If children's music stops developing over a long period, in skill, content or expressiveness, something is obviously wrong. A child may have a special difficulty to do with music or another aspect of school activity, or to do with home; the teacher's intervention may not be judged with enough care; older children may be deprived of opportunities to explore and experiment at their level. In a stimulating environment in which children are free to follow their own interests, their natural state is one of continuous development. This is as true of *all* children's music as it is of all children's mathematics and English. Of course, children with special interest and ability will develop faster and further than most, but every child is capable of reaching a certain level of musical functioning, as the examples in this book demonstrate. Most of the children we meet in primary *and* secondary schools use rhythmic ideas intuitively, that is, if they are given an opportunity to do so: but few of them pass through this stage (pre-operational thinking) to conserve ideas of time and pattern, and use them with analytical intention (operational thinking).

SUMMARY

Concrete ideas of time are the first to develop in children, beginning with pulse. After this, keeping time becomes of paramount importance, and music often consists only of beats, with the later addition of rests, dynamics, change of tempo, rolls and grace notes. Subsequently when patterning reappears, children analyse their music by counting, though at first it is the number of sounds (hits) which are counted rather than the number of beats, and they assume that music is faster if divisions of the beat are incorporated. The example of analysis set by teachers is crucial here. The notion of accent leads to the idea of beat grouping,

B

and it is important that a variety of models be presented to children. At a later stage understanding of beat divisions extends to include dotted notes, simple and compound time and irregular divisions, and the idea of stress and accent extends to include syncopation and cross-rhythm.

We underestimate the importance of children's early 'experiments' with beats and time patterns, often making premature suggestions about tunes, before the concept of pulse is truly established. This accounts for the difficulty many older children have of keeping in time, i.e. accommodating to someone else's beat.

3 Pitch

The first section of this chapter is concerned with the development of concepts of pitch; the development of pitch accuracy, in vocalising and singing, is discussed in a second section. It is important to draw a distinction between these two aspects of pitch development. In all areas of learning, conceptual development is a direct result of children's actions on the materials presented to them; at first they are involved in the muscular sensation of the action, for example banging, and later in its visual aspect, aim. It is some time later that the auditory aspect of causing a sound becomes of prime importance. On the other hand, the sensations children experience as they make vocal sounds or sing are imprecise, certainly not visible, and dependent on the growth of aural perception for their accuracy. To take the view that all children's musical activity should be based on singing, is to ignore the vital importance to children's development of their actions on materials. It is this experience which lays the foundation of conceptual structures.

As our means of measuring aural vertical space – by naming INTERVALS – is reflected in the structure of tuned percussion instruments, the importance of providing such instruments in school becomes apparent, if adequate provision is to be made for the early stages of pitch development. The skill of playing a xylophone or glockenspiel is one step further in a child's development than the skill of playing drums, and a more flexible movement has to replace the direct action of banging. The production of good tone is largely caused in the same way, though it is at first affected by the greater precision of aim necessary. The first experience of making a tune on an instrument usually occurs as the banging action learned by young children is extended in space

on a xylophone or glockenspiel; the selection of notes is at first
random, and entirely dependent on the action of banging. Many
eight and nine year olds using these instruments for the first time,
behave in exactly this way, behaviour usually found in much
younger children.

A boy (9) new in school, had had little previous musical experience;
his activity demonstrated his need to make up the experiences he had
missed. He chose all the instruments he could lay his hands on, spread-
ing them widely round him on the floor, hitting, and missing, and not
looking at what he was doing. It was a matter of chance that sometimes interesting patterns of rhythm and pitch emerged.

As rhythmic ideas are established early in most children, any
intuitively played melody is likely to be rhythmically patterned
(see Example 1). The use of patterns of pitch emerges gradually
in children's work, perhaps from the repetition of a note, or of a
short motif of notes, or from using a spatial pattern.

EXAMPLE 24   Girl (7)

As we have seen in Chapter 1, sequences are one of the first
organisations of pitch to be used by children (see Example 6).

EXAMPLE 25   Boy (7)
The rhythmic patterning made his descending figure interesting.

EXAMPLE 26   Girl (8)
She extended her sequence by INVERTING the pattern.

EXAMPLE 27   Boy (8)

He controlled his use of a sequential passage, using it to good effect.

At a later stage, when children choose their notes 'on purpose'
to make a tune, pulse and pattern may be briefly forgotten, for
it is more difficult to play tunes which do not include sequences.
At this time, children's focus is on the movement from note to
note in a melody. The slow deliberation necessary to hit the
'right' notes often seems to bring about a regression in children's
activity; even the skill of banging may seem to be lost, and
beaters, for example, may be left resting on notes after they have
sounded.

EXAMPLE 28*   Girl (9)

EXAMPLE 29*   Girl (9)

Both the tunes above took minutes to play, and no musical sense
was apparent in the playing. The audience, their own class, so
identified themselves with the two children labouring to read
from their own SCORES and hit the right notes, that they listened
attentively. When children are reaching out to encompass a new
idea, all their concentration is, for the moment, on the new aspect,
and because the musical skills already developed have yet to find
their permanent equilibrium, an apparent regression occurs.
This apparent regression marks the beginning of a new phase of
development and does not usually last for long.

Children's first analysis of the structure of tunes is usually
concerned with the movement from note to note, either by step or
leap. Early tunes are often entirely made up of stepwise motion,
for this is more easily played.

EXAMPLE 30   Girl (7)

Leaps may occur when a return is made to a starting-note or to a
recurrent note; for ease of playing this is often the top or bottom
note.

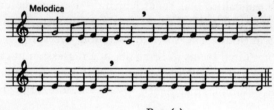

EXAMPLE 31   Boy (7)

TEACHER 'How did you organise your tune?'
CHILD (8) 'First of all hit a D and then E.'
TEACHER 'You hit D and then the next-door note.'
CHILD 'Yes.'
TEACHER 'The next one up or down?'
CHILD 'Up.'
TEACHER 'So you moved up to the next step.'
CHILD 'Yes, and then up to the next step again.'
TEACHER 'I see. You went to the second step and the third step
after your first step D.'

This discussion is obviously providing an opening for the
beginnings of an analysis of the degrees of the SCALE and the
intervals between notes. It exemplifies the teacher's role in using
a meaningful situation to take children's understanding further,
if this is judged to be appropriate. It also exemplifies the very
careful use of language necessary. On this occasion, the idea of
the second and the third step was grasped, and it was not long
before children were talking about the THIRD above a given
note instead of the third step above a first step. Using their own
general language like this, paves the way for children to learn the
technical language of our musical culture. At first, it is a general
idea of thirds which develops; a later stage brings about the
distinction between MAJOR and MINOR thirds, and this is turn
has to arise from a situation in which the focus is on the idea of

thirds. The following example illustrates the development of this idea.

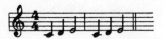

EXAMPLE 32   Girl (8)

BOY (9) 'That's the beginning of Frère Jacques.'

GIRL (9) 'Not quite.'

TEACHER 'If you have a tune instrument see if you can play that pattern.'

The 'discovery' of a tune like 'Frère Jacques' can lead – under the guidance of the teacher – to many further discoveries, this being entirely dependent on the stages of development within the class.

BOY (9) 'I've worked out the first two lines.'

He was completely stumped at working out what came next, because he could not encompass the idea of reversing the direction. He could work out tunes going up, and tunes going down, but, at that time, a tune which did both had no meaning for him. His thinking was irreversible in this situation.

TEACHER 'What note did you begin Frère Jacques on?'

BOY 'The bottom one, C.'

TEACHER 'Can you play the first line of it beginning on another note; how about G .... Now try it on F. Can you begin on F♯?'

The extensions at first were kept strictly to the KEYS in which the first three steps were either all 'black' or all 'white' notes, giving the children repeated experience of the particular and constant succession of notes, both visually and aurally. On a subsequent occasion this was taken further.

TEACHER 'What was the tune you worked out the other day?'

BOY 'Frère Jacques.'

TEACHER 'Where did you begin?'

BOY 'On C.'

GIRL (9) '*And* on G, and F♯.'

TEACHER 'Play them again; now begin on D.'

An attempt was made to do so.

BOY 'That's not right! (he had played D, E, F).

TEACHER 'But you did go to the third.'

BOY 'Yes, but it was a sort of less third.'

TEACHER 'Well, could you make it a bigger third?'

A FOURTH was played.

GIRL 'I know . . . use a black note.'

On another occasion this was extended further.

TEACHER 'Play a greater third from C. Now play a lesser third. Do the same from G.'

When it became clear that the idea had been assimilated by some of the children, the correct terminology of major and minor was given, with explanations of the Latin roots. Here were laid the foundations of an understanding of major and minor progression.

These discussions have been described in detail as they exemplify the role of the teacher in building on what children *themselves* produce and discover, bringing to their attention the ideas they have used, the naming of them, and later the notation of them, within the discipline of music. This learning was quick; other children might take longer to comprehend the ideas, though their comprehension would pass through similar stages.

The following example describes how some members of a class of seven and eight year olds were able to begin using their voices with precision; the skill developed through distinct stages. They had become familiar with the sight and sound of thirds played on xylophones and glockenspiels, and were beginning to understand the relationship between the two notes. In first attempts to pitch a third above a given note, the intermediate step was sung out loud in vocal replication of the playing of steps on an instrument; they sang ascending steps, stopping at the third. The teacher found this valuable in preparing the way for learning other intervals.

TEACHER 'Sing up to the fifth step.'

'Sing up to the seventh.'

The steps were sung within the major framework in an intuitive response to all the music they had heard and sung within this idiom.

In the previous example, children became aware of thirds from their experience of singing 'Frère Jacques'; other songs might create different starting-points, for example the interval of a FIFTH with which 'Twinkle twinkle little star' begins. However, the frequency with which the first, second and third steps of a scale appear in children's songs, and the significance of the third in major and minor TONALITY, in addition to the simplicity of the idea of three steps, makes this a most valuable starting-point for children's analysis of intervals.

A later stage in learning to pitch intervals is characterised by silent singing of intermediate steps. At first the expression on children's faces and the movements of their heads, often give a clear indication of their picturing of an instrument and the action of playing. Gradually the exact aural spacing of each interval is learned, and can be both produced at will, and recognised, when it occurs in a song or composition. It is usually later that the idea of descending steps and intervals emerges.

We have seen that childrens' first naming of the degrees of the scale is by the number of the step; this helps them to learn how to measure aural vertical space. The more sophisticated use of technical terms, TONIC, DOMINANT etc., follows once the idea and the *general* naming of it are thoroughly known by children. Given the musical environment discussed in this book, no props such as solfa are necessary, indeed, learning to pitch intervals using solfa can prevent understanding of their structuring, as it encourages a rote response. This has no place in the early stages of the conceptual development of children.

An understanding of the movement of note to note by step paves the way for the development of the notion of scale. The first idea of scale is not necessarily one in which the steps are bounded by the OCTAVE, the basic notion is of stepwise movement up and down. Children play steps going up, (downward steps usually appear later), for as long as the instrument 'lasts' (see Example 2), the length of scale, in their view, being determined by the length of the instrument. The naming of such a progression of steps presents no difficulty if children know that *scala* is the Latin for ladder. On subsequent occasions, the whole idea of scale can be discussed in a more specific and accurate manner. It is perhaps important here, to reiterate the principle of the general leading to the specific in children's learning, for it is appropriate to children's development that the word 'scale' should first be used by them in a general way: this is the essence of the concept in music. Some teachers might consider this to be inaccurate and in some way harmful, but this is to ignore the refining process of all learning: the specific and detailed develops from the general and global. The moment to draw children's attention more deeply to the structure of scales, and to encourage the more precise use of the term might arise, for example, at an intuitive finishing at the octave.

> TEACHER 'Where did you finish your scale?'
> GIRL (8) 'On C.'
> TEACHER 'You began on a C and ended on a C.'
> GIRL 'Yes.'
> TEACHER 'What step did you end on?'
> GIRL 'The eighth.'
> BOY 'The octave.'
> TEACHER 'What would happen if you continued?'
> GIRL (After a pause) 'You'd begin all over again, except you couldn't end it, because the xylophone stops at A.'

A discussion about the significance of the octave developed from this, and the teacher was requested to give a demonstration of the kind of scale-playing needed to pass exams. If no one in the class had remembered the word 'octave', the teacher would have had an opportunity to introduce the term into the discussion, in the *presence* of the idea it represents.

With some groups of children of this age, a teacher might have been able to take this further, perhaps by initiating a discussion about the different ways of travelling from one note to its octave. Nine and ten year olds quickly understand the formulae of CHROMATIC, PENTATONIC and major scales as these progressions will almost certainly have been used in their earlier work, the structure of each of these progressions being dissimilar, and easily recognisable both aurally and visually. When children are confronted with a chromatic xylophone or glockenspiel, they perceive two parts to the instrument, the row of notes near to them and the far row of notes. As a result their music often consists either of all 'white' or all 'black' notes, or of movement up one row of notes and down the other. This activity helps children to assimilate the sound of pentatonic and DIATONIC progression.

Children's first idea of a pentatonic scale is of a scale on the 'black' notes. When the recurrence of the pattern at the octave is perceived, they are ready to analyse its five-note structure and to name it by the correct term, knowing that *pentatonic* is the Greek for five notes. If suitable provision of instruments is made, i.e. fully chromatic ones, children will learn this progression as they do others, and some will choose to use it, though others may find it dull. However, the practice of presenting children with instruments tuned solely to the pentatonic scale, or perhaps with only two or three selected notes, is in direct conflict with our present knowledge of children's development, and cannot be justified on musical or educational grounds. The popularity of this method of organising children's early musical experience is perhaps due to the fact that the basic problems of technique and selection of notes in pitch and harmony are by-passed, with the result that children's music appears to be successful, and makes a pleasant sound however many are working together. But at the present time, we are beginning to understand the *vital* importance of children's early experience in establishing the concepts pertaining to particular subject disciplines and in developing technical skills in handling the requisite materials. We realise that it is not the teachers who have to solve the problems which arise in children's activities, but the children themselves: it is the development of *their* thinking and *their* ability to make informed judgements that is the main purpose of education. We must therefore create opportunities for children to learn how to choose, acknowledging that their early decisions may not coincide with ours and that in such situations in music, we have no right to expect a 'pleasant' sound. As we have seen, children's use of the pentatonic scale emerges at the time when their perception of the instrument governs their action; at a later stage it is *one* of the progressions of pitch which they use in their work (see Example 67). But if this is the only progression they meet they will be deprived of assimilatory experiences of progression by SEMITONE, and the CONSONANCE and DISSONANCE of differing CHORD patterns. This is singularly inappropriate in the twentieth century. Similarly if the notes of xylophones and glockenspiels are arranged so that they are easy to play, either by removing some or altering their position, children's perception of the technical problems of playing these instruments is prevented from developing, and their spatial awareness of the place of notes on the instrument will be a false or incomplete one.

The first use of the chromatic scale usually occurs with a

decision to play every note of an instrument, either going up or down or doing both; some children experience difficulty in perceiving the exact order of notes, and need considerable experience of hearing the progression before their ear can correct their movements.

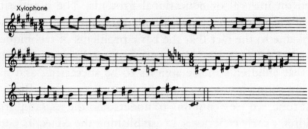

EXAMPLE 33   Girl (10)

The fact that C to C on the 'white' notes forms a major scale, and becomes a familiar sound to children in early musical experiments, fosters their understanding of this progression. The understanding is at first active and later aural, when their ears tell them that a mistake has been made. Once the formula of the progression has been understood, children have no difficulty in working out scales beginning on different notes, checking that they are right both aurally and by analysing the position of TONES and semitones. Time is necessary to work out the whole range of major scales and, according to the need of the moment, the memorising of KEY SIGNATURES will occur.

A boy (10) had become interested in playing scales on the piano. He decided to write out the whole range of scales with their fingering. The teacher helped him to begin the cycle of sharp and flat scales, giving an explanation of the TETRACHORD. When he understood these relationships he continued by himself.

Children of ten and eleven begin to understand the use of formulae and learn to apply them in various situations. Once the formula of a major scale is learned there is no problem at all in working out scales beginning on different notes; it just takes time. The idea of giving children a scale a week to learn not only wastes their time, but completely underestimates the intellectual capacity of ten and eleven year olds to apply formulae in different situations.

As the examples in this book illustrate, much of the music children compose is in major tonality; this is the inevitable result of assimilatory activity from the music they hear, the greater part of which is likely to be in major tonality.

It was on Christmas night

1 It was on Christ-mas night – – a   ba – – by was born, He was
2 His mo – ther was Ma–ry – – His   fa – – ther Jo – seph – – –
3 Now on that Christ-mas night – – three Kings they came from far – – –

born – in a sta – – ble a   ve – ry old – – – one; 4 And
And they nam'd their ba – by boy   Je – – – – – – sus;
And they brought him love-ly gifts just what I'd like to have;

if you liv'd in Beth – le – hem, you'd know – on that night,   A

ba – – by was born there, His   name was Je – sus Christ.

EXAMPLE 34   Girl (9)

The idea of a minor scale involves an alternative yet similar progression of tones and semitones to a major scale; because of this, it presents more difficulty to children and individual differences are most evident in the rate at which this idea is learned. Time is needed for the conservation of the major formula and for the visual aspect of black and white keys to cease to influence children's thinking; then the concept of minor becomes established in the same manner as the concept of major.

EXAMPLE 35   Boy (9)

Music he had heard during the previous week had been in minor tonality and he was able to accommodate to this immediately.

EXAMPLE 36*   Girl (10)

If children only use the 'white' notes of an instrument it does not necessarily mean that they are centering their music round C; other centerings result in MODAL progressions (see Example 52).

A group of twelve year olds produced a book on the history of scales. They were beginning to develop a sense of the historical growth of music.

When a tune has been played beginning on different notes the notion of TRANSPOSITION is present, as it was in the working out of 'Frère Jacques'. As the idea of different scales begins to be established, it becomes a challenge to play a tune in different keys: songs that have been known for a long time are often treated in this way. Children soon realise that this is a necessary part of musical skill, not just for its own sake, though this is part of the challenge, but because it can solve problems of pitch range.

A girl (10) composed a carol in the key of F, using the keyboard to help her. When she sang it to the class she, and everyone else, decided that it would sound better in a higher key. She sang it in A, but had difficulty with the high notes. It was then put into G and she wrote it out in the new key.

If a song is written for a particular singer, the developed and comfortable range of voice needs to be used and an appropriate key selected.

EXAMPLE 37   Girls (10)

They intuitively pitched this to suit their vocal range; it was performed on several occasions and always pitched accurately without the note being given. Getting to know a note like this can lead to a lasting knowledge of its pitch when the specific purpose is long past. Ultimately this could lead to a sense of ABSOLUTE PITCH.

EXAMPLE 38*   Girls (11)

EXAMPLE 39*   Girls (12)

In the notating of these examples instruments were used for reference, though for the most part the children were confident of their aural analysis. A discussion on ROUNDS and CANONS followed this piece of work.

The various instruments found in schools do not always have the same range of notes and are not all fully chromatic, so adjustments of key may be necessary. But quite apart from these factors, children begin to select keys for their particular effect, and an interest develops in the keys chosen by composers for works children know. Instead of expressing the idea of key by talking about the music using a particular scale, children begin to use the precise manner of talking about music written in a particular key. Children's own work at this time is often intentionally written in a chosen key.

GIRL (11) 'We have decided to write in F major.'

Her statement reflects her present focus on the idea of key: what her group wrote and what instruments were to be used was at that time far less important than using a particular key. Later these aspects once more found a truer perspective.

EXAMPLE 40*   Boy (11)

He wrote this tune with the ACCIDENTALS necessary, but needed help in deciding what key he was in.

Children's awareness of key is fostered if announcements of full title and key are given when recorded music is played to them, not only on formal occasions like Assemblies, but on every occasion.

However, to suggest that the organisation of pitch in our musical culture is wholly dependent on the diatonic system is to ignore the developments of the last hundred years. The first freeing of the rigidity of the key system and the power (and limitation) of the PERFECT CADENCE began with Impressionist experiments. The use and understanding of the WHOLE TONE scale arises naturally in children's experiments with scales: they realise that if there is a half-tone scale there must be a whole-tone scale! Children respond immediately to the fluid quality of the sound this progression produces and become interested in the Impressionist period of musical history.

A boy (10) was fascinated by the sound of the whole-tone scale; for several weeks he improvised at the keyboard using it. At first his focus was on the melodic aspect, but later a concern developed for the harmonies he produced in his playing.

There will probably be some distance in time between the first experiments with a whole-tone scale and discussions about the ideas of the Impressionists. The teacher's judgement of the assimilatory potential of the children is all important; it may be that the historical facts need to be discussed, or, if mathematical ideas are the focus, nothing more may be needed than a discussion about the formula. At such times, an opportunity to listen to the music of the period needs to be created, not for the traditional purpose of appreciation, but to feed the ear with the relevant sound, encouraging the gradual assimilation of the idiom. At a later stage, when analysis becomes more stringent, it is possible to look at this period of music far more deeply and to study the devices and harmonies used.

Ten and eleven year olds begin to be aware of the problems of the composer; in a primitive sense they have been through it all! One group of children responded to the feeling of 'trying to get away from the same old scale' and were able to understand information given to them about the work of Schoenberg and the development of SERIAL writing. Some of them felt challenged to avoid any hint of tonality in their work, and even though it

proved exceedingly difficult for them to do, they were excited at
the newness of the sound they created and its possibilities.

EXAMPLE 41*   Girls (12)

They were influenced in composing this music by the discussions they
had had on serial composition. They used a row of fifteen notes, the
last three being a retrograde of the first three; A and B were omitted
and G and B♭ repeated. The clarinet row of eight notes was based on
some of the intervals used in the longer row. By a process of augmentation and diminution each voice was given a particular movement to
suit the instrument's tone quality and the player's skill!

In looking at the composition of ten, eleven and twelve year
olds it is virtually impossible to isolate their use of pitch from the
other aspects of their music. They compose songs, and melodies

for solo instruments, but at the same time they are beginning to be concerned with producing themes capable of development, or to write short pieces which are really RHAPSODIC in nature.

EXAMPLE 42*   Girl (12)

SINGING

Singing is of course a very important part of children's musical activity; it is also another area of their development at which a more searching look needs to be taken. Even if children have had good experience in their first school (see Chapter 1), it is likely that many seven and eight year olds will not yet have learned to sing in tune. This does not mean that they never will learn to do so, but that this particular skill is taking longer to develop in their activity. Many children whose singing accuracy develops late are permanently inhibited by the reception their out-of-tune singing meets in some junior and middle schools; we are aware that these children are sometimes told not to sing or to mouth the words. Nothing is more likely to prevent the development of pitch accuracy, for apart from the emotional reaction to this treatment, children who have this difficulty need *much more* experience of singing and of hearing themselves sing: the skill cannot be learned without practice. However, most children develop this accuracy by the time they are eight or nine, indicating that the first years in a junior or middle school are a crucial time in the development of this skill, when it is finally being established.

As singing is an obvious way of beginning to work with children (see Chapter 9), it is in this activity that teachers will first be able to make observations of the stages of development of 'new' children, not in a test situation, but as they sing together informally. Children may not be able to accommodate to a specific pitch at all, or the song may be out of the developed range of their voice. As the range of young children's voices is lower than is usually considered, it is obviously necessary to begin singing songs with them in C or D, or perhaps lower, in order to pinpoint the problem of reproducing pitch accurately.

A class of thirty-five seven and eight year olds sang *The drummer and the cook* in D. Nine children were not singing it accurately, but when it came to the chorus line which rises to the upper tonic the incidence of inaccuracy greatly increased. Furthermore, singing B^I, $C\sharp^{II}$ and D^{II} was so far beyond some children's range that they lost all sense of relative pitch and began a high-pitched drone.

Choosing a song in which such a rise in pitch occurs, or singing the same song in different keys, gives teachers a clear indication of the levels of pitch accuracy and ranges of voice of the children in a class; indeed, the choice of songs should be made with this in mind. This also applies to the choice of songs for older children, for some eleven and twelve year olds have developed only a limited range of pitch, while some of the boys' voices may be breaking. Their needs must be considered alongside those of children whose range is much greater.

A group of girls (11) composed a song in A major so that one of their friends could be in their group and join in the singing. Her ability to reproduce pitch accurately had only recently developed to a range of A to A^I; for most of her middle years she had been unable to sing in tune but had been working with her teacher to extend her vocal range.

If children are to develop their singing potential, they need frequent opportunities to sing in school: one lesson a week is not enough. Seven, eight and nine year olds really need to spend a short time singing on most days. This means that class teachers can share in the activity with children and sing with them in the classroom, even though there may be time-tabled music lessons with a specialist as well. But it is not enough to sing through familiar songs and old favourites week after week, as happens in many schools. Children need to be involved in their own development, they need to be aware of their developing skill in the reproduction of pitch and range of voice, in tone quality and resonance, in enunciation and breath control, in INTONATION, in part-singing and in following a conductor. Clearly, singing time should include discussions of the song chosen and discussion and practice of the problems arising in it; the points raised by teachers and pinpointed for practice should be within children's possible level of skill and understanding. Children's first active acquaintance with our musical culture is in singing tunes, or snatches of tunes, they have heard. From this experience, and their experience of listening to music, the first intuitive ideas of phrasing, cadence, and melodic shape develop. The more they sing, and the greater the variety of melodic styles they encounter, the richer their early assimilatory experience will be; this in turn affects the quality of their later learning. These principles apply to children's work throughout the middle school.

Teachers' knowledge of children's instrumental music helps them to make decisions about possible ideas for discussion in singing time. For example, when it is apparent that children are becoming aware of the importance of ending music, teachers can foster this development by drawing attention to the end of a song, perhaps by getting slower, or quieter or keeping the last note on for a long time. If the idea of sequences has emerged in children's work, songs with sequential passages need to be chosen. Songs also need to be chosen which 'feed in' new ideas as well as using ones which are emerging in children's work.

The inner drive to do things better and better which is evident in children's behaviour affects their singing activity, if it has not been put off course by the endless repetition of songs to which little attention is paid.

TEACHER (to class of eight year olds) 'Did you notice any part of that song that we ought to practise?'
BOY 'Yes, the bit where it jumped – "We sailed around the world".'
The teacher sang some pitch patterns for the children to copy, which included leaps of an octave. The interval which had caused difficulty was incorporated into short phrases which were used as exercises, meeting the needs of the occasion. After a few minutes the song was sung again, with improvement in the passage which had been practised.

Difficult intervals, the intonation of repeated notes, the pronunciation of vowels and consonants, and other problems arising in songs, can be used as exercises in this way; they may be made up by the teacher or by the children. The practice point should not always be selected by the teacher but decided on in discussion with the children, as the above example illustrates. Not only do such improvised exercises help to solve problems of pitch accuracy and singing technique, but they also help children's musical memory to develop.

A class of ten year olds used their recorders in a discussion. They copied a short tune played by the teacher or by one of the class; they did this individually and the listeners gave assistance if inaccuracies occurred.

Teachers can foster the development of children's vocal range by improvising 'stretching' exercises, playing and experimenting with sounds; to sing confidently and well children need to know what their voices can do. The following sounds and short FIGURES of pitch were given to a class of seven and eight year olds to copy for this purpose.

EXAMPLE 43

Formally organised singing lessons in which children sit or stand in rows, often prevent children from focusing on the matter in hand; they may be too tense to be able to produce good tone and to function at their best, and if they are seated in rows of desks, they will feel vocally isolated from each other. These problems do not arise if children are grouped round the teacher as they might be to listen to a story; the younger ones will not need chairs, but seating will probably be necessary for the older ones. On the other hand, it is almost impossible to establish a close working relationship with children if the teacher is a remote, and perhaps worried, figure at the keyboard. Furthermore, the piano often proves to be a stumbling block in the way of children's vocal development for if their singing is constantly accompanied, they are prevented from developing a vocal independence and a fine perception of intonation; children who have difficulty in the accurate reproduction of pitch cannot hear where they are inaccurate, and are forced by circumstances to go on singing out of tune. Unaccompanied singing is therefore essential for the development of pitch accuracy and vocal independence; it is appropriate throughout children's development that teachers should not be tied to the keyboard, but in close relation to children as they work in a group. Of course, children need experience of being accompanied when they sing songs which they have learned, whether they are singing to themselves or to other people, but if they are learning to be vocally independent, it should not be necessary for the accompaniment to double the melody line.

When children are gathered round the teacher singing songs and working at problems which have arisen, they are experiencing what was once time-tabled as aural training, but in a lively and meaningful way as the points dealt with are relevant to their present activity and very much in their minds. Teachers can foster the development of aural perception and vocal skill by extending the points which need practice; the patterns of time and pitch to be reproduced can be made longer, the patterning more complex, and the use of pitch range more taxing. The familiar activities of melodic IMPROVISATION, the use of question and answer phrases, conducting the discussion in RECITATIVE, exploring the rhythms of words, all serve to enrich children's aural perception and vocal experience. When they have learned to analyse the basic components of time and pitch patterns, to describe this verbally, and to write and read notation, then they are ready to learn how to take dictation. Obviously the ideas and the instruments used to introduce this activity should be ones very familiar to the children; books of aural tests do not meet the needs of children who are acquiring this skill. Moreover there is very little point in testing skills before they have developed, though this has been traditional practice for many years!

The use of song books also needs to be considered in relation to children's development. At first they will learn songs from memory, copying what the teacher sings; if their attention is focused, *at their level*, on the problems arising, this activity should be more than a rote one. Later, when they are beginning to learn notation, the surge of interest in scores naturally extends to the music of the songs they learn. But it is not enough to hand round the books and go through the songs; children want to know what every sign means, and much time needs to be spent in discussion of signs which are new to them. At a later stage they will be able to tackle the problem of singing at sight; the growth of this skill is fostered if children themselves are sometimes responsible for making up some of the tunes for sight-singing. This does not always have to be organised in the group discussion time, but can continue when the children are organising their own work, for they are challenged to become skilful at sight-singing just as they were challenged at a much earlier stage to become skilful at hitting a drum.

SUMMARY

Children's early actions on instruments lay the foundation of conceptual structures. Experience of tuned percussion instruments is desirable in pitch development, as their construction reflects our system of naming intervals. These should be fully chromatic, since such restrictions as pentatonic tuning bypass problems of dissonance and resolution, and retard musical development. Tunes are first made by random banging; this gives way to the use of repetition and sequence, and later, to tunes which move more freely. Children first analyse tunes according to the movement by step or leap, and from this, ideas of scale and interval emerge. At first these are general ideas, which gradually become more specific and concerned with the particular progressions of major, pentatonic, chromatic and minor scales, and modes, and particular types of interval. In discussion, children's own language gives way to the use of terminology, if teachers present terms meaningfully and often. Learning the exact pitch of notes results from practice and performance of songs composed, which are often transposed to suit particular singers, thus deepening understanding of key. The spiral of learning leads to further ideas of progression at a later stage, in whole tone and serial experiments.

Pitch accuracy is usually developed by the age of eight or nine. Children who have difficulty in accommodating to specific pitch need more vocal opportunities than do the others. This skill is fostered by first pitching songs in the developed range, and later, by singing in various keys or choosing songs of extended range. The singing should usually be unaccompanied and the atmosphere relaxed. Weekly sing-songs invariably blunt children's vocal development, and make little contribution to their general development in music. Singing activity should be an integral part of work in music and the choice of repertoire and points for discussion should be linked to instrumental work.

FURTHER READING

Cleall, Charles   *Voice Production in Choral Technique*   Part 3
    Novello, 1969
Franklin, Erik   *Music Education: Psychology and Method*
    Harrap, 1972 (pp. 74–5)

4 Form

Shape and form give meaning to artistic expression. In musical expression rhythm, melody, and harmony are organised to form a coherent whole; they are the component parts which are communicated to the listener by means of the overall plan. Children's early experiments with sound lack the organisation which would make them coherent to an adult, and it takes time for this to develop. As we have seen, the action itself is of supreme importance at first, and absorbs children's whole attention. Small snatches of coherence may emerge in their work, only to be lost again almost at once. As they begin to think operationally, children become more aware of the sound they are making, and of other children's reaction to it, and they begin to realise how important the planning of music is. Ways of ending are usually the first to be considered; a loud bang in music in which beats are the focus, or a slide in a tune on a pitch instrument, are the early means employed to make good endings. A loud bang or a glissando have the same significance for an eight year old as a perfect cadence has for a musician. Most eight year olds understand that endings are important.

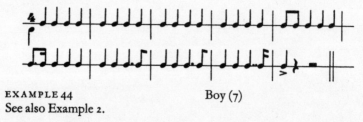

EXAMPLE 44   Boy (7)
See also Example 2.

While children are at different stages in their understanding of how to end a piece of music, some of the others in the class may find it intolerable to listen to music which continues endlessly; the music of many eight and nine year olds does this if they do not yet feel the need to bring music to a satisfactory close. On one occasion yells of 'Stop!' from the other children barely caused a seven year old to halt in his tracks; a group of nine year olds had more consideration for the feelings of a newcomer who had not had music lessons in school before, and tried to explain the importance of ending to him. Given appropriate early school experience, the basic concepts of pulse and form (beginning and ending) should be developed in eight year olds. Teachers need to assess the levels of understanding of these concepts in children for it is with them that notions of form begin.

GIRL (8) 'I am keeping in 2 time; J is in 2 time; K is in 4 time; then we all get slower and slower and we die away.'

When children choose to work together it becomes necessary to plan how they will end at the same time. At first nudges are used as a signal, and are later refined into meaningful looks! When children have coped with the problem of ending satisfactorily (at their level), attention is turned to the beginning: up till this time the music has begun in response to the teacher's request that a child, or group of children, should play to the class. Ways of beginning music are not intrinsically musical, but are forms of organisation which equally apply to other arts, and indeed to everyday life. In music, all the players can begin together, or they can each play in turn, or they can begin one after another in staggered entry. These methods of beginning are explored by children, and signals are used for a concerted entry; e.g. 'one, two, three, Go!' or 'ready, steady, Go!'

A group of eight year olds came in at a vigorous nod from the leader. The signal and the ending were the only planned parts in the music; the rest was an improvisation and the patterning was intuitive.

A method of beginning frequently employed by children is for one member of the group to establish the beat, creating a rhythmic introduction for the other players.

GIRL (8) irritatedly (playing beats) 'Come *in*!'
PARTNER 'I like to wait until I've got the beat in my head.'

EXAMPLE 45   Girls (9)

Experience of organising music so that the players enter in turn, whether or not a solo part finally enters as in the example above, leads toward the idea of a more precise form of staggered entry in which the players enter with the same theme. Example 68 is of a round composed by a group of ten year old girls: they found it difficult to sustain the COUNTERPOINT all the way through and so organised it in two sections. In Example 41, twelve year old girls used a more sophisticated means of staggered entry: they entered imitatively, each voice having the same notes but a different rhythmic scheme (see Chapter 3).

As they play and listen to each other, children's attention becomes once more directed to the manner of ending a piece of music: they become aware of the need for *suitable* endings. There comes a point when they realise that bangs and slides are rather primitive means of ending, and are not convincing if there is no connection with what has gone before. Nevertheless, these ways of ending are still used by older children, even when the content of their music has become more sophisticated.

Two girls (7) played random notes on melodicas; when they happened to play a major third which resolved the preceding major SECOND, they stopped. The rest of the class were audibly satisfied with this.

A group of nine and ten year olds heard this music played.

EXAMPLE 46

BOY (9) 'I think it should have a glissando at the end.'

Several children burst out 'Oh no!' The teacher suggested that it should be performed again, finishing with a glissando. Nobody liked the result; the original had a musically satisfactory ending, if not a strong one. But the ending itself was not the boy's concern: he was practising how to select material from his store of musical ideas which was relevant to the present situation. It was important that he should hear his suggested ending, even though the other children could imagine the result.

Putting a loud bang on the end of a piece of music has its parallel in musical form. Apart from the obvious link with a loud TONIC CHORD, or several loud tonic chords at different pitches, additional material can be added to strengthen the close of a work in the form of a CODA (literally tail-piece). Works with such additions need to be played to children, and of course discussed, when this direction of development becomes apparent in their music.

It is only when beginnings and endings are sorted out that children perceive that the working out of the 'middle' (children's language) is important too. Children of eight and nine have not always learned to retrace their steps mentally, and to play their music at all they have to begin at the beginning and play it through until the end. If a mistake is made (a mistake in relation to their intention which *they* know but is not always easy for the teacher to construe) the usual comment is 'Can I go back to the beginning?'

A girl (9) stumbled and stopped in a piece of music for glockenspiel.

GIRL 'Can I go back to the beginning?'

TEACHER 'Try to pick it up where you left off.'

The child looked completely blank; she made some attempts to do so but with no success.

GIRL 'I can't.'

TEACHER 'Right then, go back to the beginning as you suggested.'

Children's irreversible thinking reinforces their early focus on beginnings and endings: they are the parts of music which can be held in mind. But as their thinking becomes more mobile, they learn to hold in mind and retrace the steps taken during their work. This is an enormous step forward in their musical functioning, for the idea of a whole piece of music and its parts can then be considered.

A girl (9) on her third visit to a music workshop played a pattern of three descending notes as a descending sequence on a xylophone. The teacher suggested that the pattern could be reversed. The child was nonplussed and spent several minutes trying out possible actions in the air. Then with a flash of inspiration she picked up the instrument, turned it round and began playing with the same action in space that she used before! She had not yet learnt to reverse her action.

When children begin to act with a definite idea in mind, remembering the time and pitch patterns they have used, it becomes possible to repeat these patterns; repetition becomes the first mode of developing a musical idea. However, the judicious use of it takes time to develop: at first, a pattern can be repeated so much that the attention of the audience is stretched to its limit. The seven year old in Example 15 continued his playing until he could carry on no longer, and then made a final effort to make a good ending; he had long since lost the attention of the class.

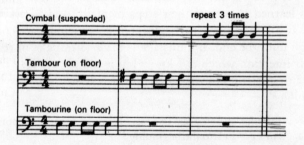

EXAMPLE 47. Music by the same boy one month later. The use of repetition was better controlled, but the music was not played in time throughout.

The reaction of their peer group is very important to children, the natural pressure they bear on each other contributes to their development. The fact that they are at similar stages of development and using the language of music in a similar way, brings about the genuine exchange of ideas and opinions. In Example 15 the reaction of the peer group drew the composer's attention to the need for greater control of repetition, and gave the teacher an opportunity to discuss and play examples of the treatment of the 'middle' and the use of repetition.

EXAMPLE 48   Girls (8)

In the examples above, patterns were repeated; they were nearly all one BAR patterns, short enough for children learning to repeat an idea, to do so exactly. The repetitions used in an OSTINATO or GROUND are relieved by the varying material played at the same time (see Examples 64 and 94), and in children's early use of sequence the effect of homing to the octave counteracts the tedium of repetitions; the judicious use of sequence also takes time to develop. As memory skill and pattern-making develop, and when music begins to be written down, the patterns which children repeat may last for two or three bars; they may not be repeated exactly. This reflects a new level of intuitive awareness of the need for variation and balance in phrases. The teacher's specific contribution here, in using the word 'phrase' in comment and discussion on every meaningful occasion, helps children to understand this further category of musical structure as distinct from the idea of bar or pattern; in children's language the word 'part' is often used to name these three ideas (bar, pattern, phrase), and others.

EXAMPLE 49   Girls (8)

EXAMPLE 50   Boy (9)

Gradually the planning of music is extended to include parts/ phrases/sections which together make up the whole, but which are not necessarily complete in themselves. Phrase patterns used

EXAMPLE 51

EXAMPLE 51 (cont.)   Girls (11)

in our musical culture appear in an intuitive response to music
children have heard, for example AABA, ABAB, AAAB (see
Examples 37, 38, 49, 50). Once the notion of separate phrases
making up a whole piece of music has been learned, children
begin to analyse the phrase structure of music they hear; discussions following a performance may often include phrase analysis.
Learning the shorthand method of expressing this using capital
letters presents no problem, for it is logical and quick. At first,
children's compositions are not begun with a particular phrase
structure in mind, though later this is often a self-imposed task
and perhaps has a place as a set task at the top of the middle
school, but usually, when the composer sees the direction his
music is taking, he follows, and works to the plan which is
growing out of the music.

C

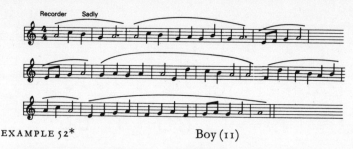

EXAMPLE 52*   Boy (11)

In the previous examples symmetrical and asymmetrical phrasing was used. The balance of phrases in our musical culture has varied historically, though children are likely to have heard music with symmetrically balanced phrase structure. Where possible, music which is constructed differently should be played to them, to fill any gaps in the range of music they have heard. To suggest directly, or indirectly through the selection of music to which they listen, that phrases are necessarily of equal length and symmetrically balanced, is limiting and inaccurate.

The idea of the extension of phrases grows from the same source as the idea of coda: an addition is made. An ending phrase may be extended for climactic effect and convincing close. As the interim section is usually the last to be considered deeply, extensions of middle phrases occur at a later stage. When this happens means are used to elaborate the 'middle' which have been successfully applied to endings and beginnings. Children's experiments with sequences often result in the extension of phrases. The use of phrase contraction develops in a similar way, often appearing first in unexpectedly shorter, and therefore effectively surprising, ending phrases, or through a mistake in timing.

EXAMPLE 53   Girls (10)
The last phrase is doubled in length for climactic effect.

EXAMPLE 54*   Girls (11)

The second phrase is contracted as a result of the overlapping of the first two phrases.

    Simple repetition, even when it is of whole sentences made up of different phrases, does not satisfy children for long: the idea of repeating material with slight differences emerges. To a rhythm may be added a roll; the dynamics may be altered; the tune may be played on different instruments or ornamented with TRILLS or glissandi. These ideas reflect a growing awareness that new material is essential to the survival of a piece of music – as long as it 'fits' (children's language), and so the idea of developing music continues to grow. The task of teachers is to note all these happenings and make specific contributions in discussion about the use of the same devices by composers with whose music the children are familiar, and to play or sing music in which the devices are used. The way in which children use these devices at first, is not necessarily successful; they may seem tacked on, contributing nothing to the coherence of the music. As children seek new and more sophisticated ways of organising musical material, they will inevitably use them clumsily at first; it is a matter of experience and practice to begin using such devices effectively. The clumsy and halting, and seemingly inappropriate, precede the more refined and coherent use of the language of music. The following list of ways of developing a theme was prepared by a group of ten and eleven year olds.

1   UNISON statement of theme, then parts to split.
2   Theme on glockenspiel, then recorders unison, then others.
3   Use the KEY-CHORD.
4   Alter dynamics and tempo.
5   Add ORNAMENTS.
6   Unison statement, then entry in order of pitch.
7   Change key, add accidentals.
8   Use different harmonies.
9   Use scale passages and CONTRARY MOTION.
10   Use of dissonance.
11   Use voices.
12   Repeat.
13   Phrase extension; sequence.
14   Inversion, RETROGRADE movement.
15   Treat as a round.

The suggestions were made in a general discussion and were later written out and kept on the wall for reference. *All* of them were ideas which had arisen in the children's own work; the teacher had given more and more precise information about musicians' use of them as the children's understanding developed. The list was meaningful for the children because they had all experienced, in some measure, the need to deal with musical ideas in the ways listed, but to put such a list on display for children who lack experience of the problems of organising music would be of little value; without concrete experience, no abstraction of essential musical concepts can take place. The children who listed the ideas were able to weigh the advantages and disadvantages of different ideas, and make judgements about their relevance in certain musical situations. They had reached the stage of abstract thinking and were able to operate within the laws of our musical discipline. It must be borne in mind that when these ideas first arise, only the most basic ingredients are present, and the sophistication of chord relationships and key relationships may not be understood. This does not mean that the ideas are inaccurately used, but rather that children's use of them is at its starting point. For children the significance which is attached to these ideas in our culture develops gradually.

In the following example a twelve year old set out to write episodes for melodica; they are not completely successful yet reflect very clearly his developing ideas about the structuring of music.

EXAMPLE 55*   Boy (11)

TERNARY organisation readily suggests itself to children, and occurs early on in the planning of music. When they have used one idea and have gone to something new for interest's sake, the idea of a return to the beginning section seems logical and satisfying; there is a relaxation in going back to familiar material which rounds off a piece of music, both for the composer-players and the audience. When children are encompassing the idea of ternary form, they have no difficulty in understanding the extended version of it in RONDO form; opportunity to listen to rondos fosters their growing understanding of the necessary balance of known and new material in composition. However the key relationship of strict ternary form may not be understood by children, even at the top of the middle school; this will again depend on how early meaningful musical experience began for them. This understanding obviously links with their learning about the CIRCLE of fifths which usually leads to discussions on key relationships. To understand the precise formula developed historically, children need experience of *playing* and listening to music written in ternary form.

EXAMPLE 56   Boys (10, 11)

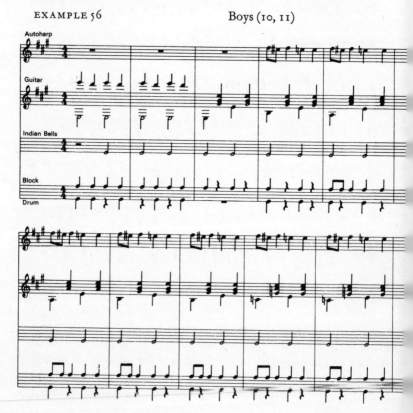

The intention of the boys in the above example was to compose in ternary form. They were delighted to have achieved this, though in doing so they almost came to blows! In their music the idea of new material providing a contrast between two repetitions of an idea is of the utmost importance: this is, after all, the essence of the form. The more sophisticated BINARY idea seldom emerges until later, conflicting, as it does, with a natural wish to return to familiar material.

The development of a concern for solo parts and accompaniments is largely due to the social development of children and the groups in which they choose to work. In each group there is usually a leader who organises the rest of the children; at seven or eight the leaders will probably be children who have developed further in their understanding and use of pitch than the rest of the group, who may still be concerned with time pattern and pulse, and *ad hoc* rather than intentional use of pitch. Music creates a marvellous opportunity for children at different stages of development to work together, with results that are satisfying to all of them, and they all learn in such a situation. The leader of the group is in a strong position to provide the solo part while the others, or the partner, provide the accompaniment ('backing' in modern parlance). A tune may be accompanied by a set of rhythms or glissandi or a repeated idea may be used (see Examples 48 and 51). Providing an accompaniment, even if it has no pitch content, is a tricky business: decisions have to be made about the suitability of the ideas chosen, and children have to fit in with each other, keep in time, and match dynamics. The balance of parts also has to be considered: 'A solo is no good if it is drowned'. Most rhythm instruments have a loud tone and this creates difficulties if the melodic instrument chosen is a glockenspiel; it may be Hobson's choice if all the other melodic instruments are being used! This experience builds up ideas of structure and balance; the way the accompaniment is given to various instruments builds the first simple ideas of ORCHESTRATION: judgements have to be made about the 'going-together' of the instruments chosen and the suitability of material for the particular expressiveness of an instrument.

EXAMPLE 57*   Boy (11)

The idea of multiple form is a sophisticated one, for it involves the putting together of separate movements to form an integrated whole.

A group of nine year olds were inspired by Holst's 'Planets Suite' and the electronic music of a T.V. series about space, to compose their own planets suite. The movements stood well on their own; the only linking factor was the programme.

It is to be expected that first attempts at multiple form will be based on a concrete idea, for the idea of programme supports the growth of a multiplicity of movements. An awareness of contrasting movements develops from music planned in ternary form as the middle section of this in children's music is often slow, and concerned with melody, whereas the surrounding sections have a more rhythmic and energetic quality. The parallel with contrasting movements of a SYMPHONY is understood by children, and though their capacity for perceiving the specific relationships between movements is not developed, contrast of mood is felt and changes in tempo are perceived. In school, there is often no opportunity to listen to whole symphonies, and concerts organised for children rarely give this opportunity. But listening to a whole work is not essential to the musical development of twelve and thirteen year olds, for not many of them will have reached the advanced stage of musical understanding necessary to construe the significance of symphonic structure. Nor is it a disservice to music if children only hear part of a symphony or similar large work, for their concentration span varies considerably and on some occasions the end of a single movement may not be reached. However, their listening experience needs to include movements of symphonies, and the detail given in announcing the music is very relevant. After much experience of listening to movements of symphonies, children can draw conclusions about the structure. They will notice that symphonies have a slow movement, usually second in order in the classical symphony; that very fast movements were included post Haydn and Mozart, and are extremely fast in some of Shostakovich's writing; that first movements are concerned with thematic development and are in a general ternary form; that modern symphonies do not always have four movements; that voices are used in some; that the orchestra is used differently in different periods of musical history. Children can only come to such conclusions if their experience of listening has been sufficiently varied for these ideas to be assimilated, and if teachers have fostered this development by drawing children's attention to what they have heard.

Groups of children may combine to compose movements to be played consecutively as a whole. The music of Example 58 was composed by a group of eleven and twelve year old girls in a music hobbies period of an hour weekly – with self-imposed homework when a tune needed to be worked out. The central themes were chosen and worked out in discussion; the instrumentation was decided as the story unfolded musically, and the voice parts were allotted according to range. Separate sections were worked out by different children at different times, but if something was found to be unsuitable it was rejected: the children realised that unity of idea was essential if the story was going to be effectively set. The overture contained the main themes and set a sombre mood; the forms used were recitative and ARIA with interjected small solo parts – they decided against a chorus proper, for they were all very concerned with solo singing and ensemble. The opera lasted for seventeen minutes. The words and actions, and above all the music, communicated the pathos and sadness of the story to the audience.

EXAMPLE 58 'The Little Snow Girl.' Girls (11, 12)

SUMMARY

Children's early musical experiments lack coherence, for it is not until operational thinking begins to develop that the planning of music is considered. The need for a satisfactory ending is the first to be felt, and until more sophisticated ideas emerge, loud bangs or glissandi are used. Children's focus then shifts to ways of beginning, by concerted, staggered or imitative entry, and signals are given for stopping and starting. As their thinking becomes reversible, they can retrace their steps mentally and begin to consider the 'middle' of their music. Repetition and sequence (endless at first), ostinato and ground gradually emerge. As a need is felt for subtler patterning, two- or three-bar patterns appear in which each bar is varied. This leads to an awareness of the structure of phrases and whole sentences, and to the use of phrase extension and contraction. Both symmetrical and asymmetrical balance of phrasing is found in children's music, and they need to listen to music structured in these ways. A subsequent stage is concerned with the sections of a piece, loosely organised into episodes, or more carefully into variation, ternary or perhaps binary form. The idea of programme is often the linking factor in first attempts to use more than one movement, and organising instrumental accompaniments to solo parts helps to lay the foundation of ideas about orchestration. In all these aspects of form children's first understanding is a general one and the ideas may be used clumsily. Subsequently they begin to perceive the fuller significance and specific construction of these forms, and others, and use them with greater skill in their compositions.

FURTHER READING

Paynter, John, and Aston, Peter   *Sound and Silence*
   C.U.P., 1970 (pp. 226–31)

5 Harmony

The first harmonic sounds produced by young children are usually the result of their action on an instrument; by using two or more beaters, or several fingers at a time on a keyboard, notes are sounded simultaneously.

EXAMPLE 59   Boy (6)

EXAMPLE 60   Boy (7)

If two children work together, playing pitch instruments, they will make a CONTRAPUNTAL sound because they are playing their tunes at the same time. Harmonic sound is initially the inadvertent result of children's actions, whether or not time and pitch pattern are present, or even perceived by the player.

The growth of the idea of pulse often results in one beater being used by children to keep time; the lowest note of an instrument is frequently chosen for this purpose as it is easy to aim for without looking, once its position has been judged. The fact that many school instruments have C as the bottom note and are tuned in C, means that a TONIC PEDAL is the result of this action.

Left-handed children sometimes reverse this activity, producing an inverted pedal.

EXAMPLE 61   Girl (7)

EXAMPLE 62   Boy (8)

He had mastered stepwise movement and was experimenting with leaps. His intention was to miss out one note each time, though he had to accommodate to the length of the instrument when he reached the top. There was no hesitation when the same problem occurred at the bottom of the instrument after the descent. He repeated the idea using fourths instead of thirds.

When this particular organisation of pitch has become part of children's knowing, the term pedal and its Latin root needs to be given. This first use of a supporting bass idea also gives an opportunity for teachers to introduce the general idea of a ground bass, the meaning of the word itself underlining its musical use.

EXAMPLE 63   Boys (9)

This was notated at pitch to avoid confusing children who were learning to relate notes to their position on the STAVE.

The idea of one part providing a ground is often used by children when they begin to organise their work in pairs or in larger groups; a need is felt to have a constant factor in the music which the players *know* and with which all the other ideas can fit. The ground has to be a short one if it is to be remembered, and this will be necessary if a written record of the music is not yet kept. The use of ostinato arises for similar reasons, especially if children choose instruments of a similar pitch range.

BOY (8) (To teacher) 'Shall I tell you how we've done it? I start like this' (playing a glissando up and down a xylophone). 'Then M. plays' (slides on a xylophone) 'louder, because the trumpet comes in and he must hear what he's doing. I can't be sure that I get it (trumpet) right.'

GIRL (8) 'It slips.'

BOY 'Then we cross over; the xylophone keeps playing hard.'

EXAMPLE 64   Boy (10)
His use of ground is more sophisticated.

The first plans to make parts fit are usually to do with timing, bringing into use ideas already firmly established, i.e. endings and beginnings. At this time the tuning-in of ending notes becomes important in children's work, and in this way cadence points begin to be considered vertically and in detail, whereas the harmony of the whole piece of music is the result of putting together several parts horizontally, with no concern for the precise intervals used. Harmony is conceived POLYPHONICALLY at first and the effect of consonance and dissonance is felt incidentally.

EXAMPLE 65*   Boy (10)

EXAMPLE 66*   Girls (10)

Their concern was to develop the four-note figure and end in unison.

EXAMPLE 67*   Boy (11)

His concern was the idea of contrary motion, and learning to play it quickly.

The green past-ures are green to - day, the cows are joy-f'lly eat - ing hay

The hor - ses are neigh-ing, the child - ren are play - ing, the pigs are a

grunt - ing (grunting) And the dogs are bark - - ing.

EXAMPLE 68*

This round was composed by a group of ten year old girls. The parts caught up after the second line, and though this was unsatisfactory to them, they could not solve the problem as they did not perceive that the metre was causing the difficulty. The parts then split again and the round ended in unison. The harmony was part intuitively and part intentionally based on the tonic TRIAD. These children had sung many rounds organised in this way and understood the harmonic structure.

Melodicas are very useful for children's early experiments with harmony as the keys are narrow enough for young children to play several notes at once, playing larger intervals than they could on the piano. Instruments need to be available for children's use on which chords can be played even more easily, for example, by pressing a button. There is pleased recognition when familiar chord patterns are produced by pressing a bar or button, for diatonic harmony is familiar to young children – most of the music they hear, of whatever type, is in this idiom. At first the spatial arrangements of the bars on an autoharp, and the groups of strings on a chordal dulcimer, or the buttons on a piano accordion, cause the harmonic progression and this music is satisfying to children until, in an intuitive response to tonality, they begin to demand a feeling of close. Then an active search for the right ending chord begins, as did the search for the right note for ending a tune.

A boy (8) played the chord of G major followed by C major.

'They went together.'

This experience establishes the beginning of an understanding of cadences.

EXAMPLE 69   Girl (8)

A search also begins for the right chords to harmonise songs that children know; ARPEGGIOS are used as accompaniments (the action of a glissando on an autoharp), not at first because the idea itself seems a good one, but because the action of playing a slide on an instrument is known, and its sound enjoyed, by children. Even beaters may be used for this purpose at first, but after the head of the beater has caught between the strings on several occasions, interrupting the flow of the glissando, a finger or plectrum is used! In accompanying songs they have made up themselves, children need not be limited to traditional harmony and can experiment with different chord constructions and progressions. When harmonic perception is beginning to develop, they need experience of singing with simple chordal accompaniments in both traditional and modern idiom. To ensure the broadest possible experience of harmony, both diatonic and 'modern' experiments need to be fostered by teachers, and music played to children which employs a variety of harmonic styles.

EXAMPLE 70   Girls (9)

They were interested in the idea of 'wrong' chords; this lead to discussions on BITONALITY and POLYTONALITY.

The melodica is particularly useful for building triads as small hands can play the first, third and fifth of a scale simultaneously, if not the octave. When triads are played beginning on different notes, children may not perceive the resultant mixture of major and minor chords (because 'white note' chords usually appear first), and it will probably be necessary for the idea of 'greater' and 'lesser' thirds to have been learned before they perceive the difference between a major and a minor chord, and learn to recognise the sound of each. Other finger patterns on a keyboard are also explored and a response to dissonance ('clashes' in children's language) becomes apparent; some children find clashes exciting, while others cover their ears at the sound. However, they accept discord as part of the harmonic structure of music with none of the difficulty experienced by many adults. Children's ears are receptive to the harmonic sound of their own time, and dissonance is accepted by them as part of the language of music. Naturally, some children find dissonance uncomfortable, whereas others find their own musical expression in harmony of this type. This does not mean that all children cannot learn to take a reasonable and informed attitude to twentieth-century harmony.

GIRL (10) 'It depends on the music you are making up. Sometimes it is right, but not always.'

From these experiences a sense of harmonic style develops, chords seeming appropriate to children in some places but not in others, or seeming appropriate to a particular musical purpose, depending on the effect wanted or the idiom chosen.

EXAMPLE 71   Girls (10)

A discussion on chords built in fourths followed this piece of work;
in the next lesson, it was played with the second part transposed up a
SEVENTH.

The children who composed Example 39 knew that the effect
would be dissonant if they sang it as a round. They practised it
many times before they were satisfied with their accuracy; only
then were they ready to discuss the interpretation of it.

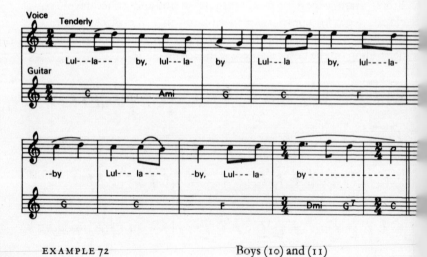

EXAMPLE 72   Boys (10) and (11)

The leader in this composition was the guitarist. He knew the chords he was playing, but did not yet understand their significance within the key. The melody line was improvised over the accompaniment.

A boy (10) used his work-time for nearly two months in experiments on a piano-accordion (fortunately nobody else wanted it!); he worked out the ordering of the buttons and the chord progressions created. Not all the music he produced was very satisfactory until his aural experience of the progressions had been sufficient for him to assimilate their sound. He spent some time putting I IV V accompaniments to simple songs in different keys (using the next set of buttons). His work led to a general discussion in his class (eleven and twelve year olds) about the use of PRIMARY TRIADS: other children produced similar accompaniments on the piano, on the autoharp and by using three beaters on a xylophone. They were given the terms tonic, dominant and SUBDOMINANT with explanation of their derivation. They were also given the system of using Roman numerals as a shorthand for describing chords. An eleven year old girl who learnt the guitar, raised the question of A^7 and this led to further discussion about V^7 and its subsequent use in composition. When the ten year old had had his fill of the piano-accordion he wrote this piece for melodicas.

EXAMPLE 73*   Boy (10)

A boy (10) perceived the cadence relationship of V–I which he had met in many piano pieces. After a discussion and demonstration of the frequency with which these two chords are used, the teacher gave him simple tunes to harmonise with I and V.

EXAMPLE 74*   Girls (10)

EXAMPLE 75   Girls (11)

EXAMPLE 76*   Boy (12)

This was written for the school choir. His attempt at writing harmony for voices was largely based on his experience of chord positions on the piano as well as on his experience of singing in three parts.

The mathematical explanations of consonance and dissonance greatly interest children of ten and eleven; they are fascinated by the science of sound and are at a stage when they can comprehend the scientific and mathematical principles involved. Time needs to be devoted to research into the science of sound, perhaps with help from a scientist on the staff. It is also an appropriate time to link with the handicraft teacher in making instruments, provided of course the *use* of the instruments is the ultimate goal and the children are sufficiently interested in making them to correct specifications.

Three boys (10) experimented with a tape-recorder in a break-time following a music lesson. They taped the sound of a cork being drawn from a bottle; conventional instruments, played in an amazing variety of unconventional ways, and various odds and ends, were also used as sound sources. They played the tape at different speeds, and 'discovered' the octave relationship between a frequency and its double. They made up their own symbols for the score as it was impossible to use traditional notation.

As our children are in school *today*, today's music, the sound of it and the look of it on paper, should be part of their experience. This means that many teachers will have some learning of their own to do if they are to catch up with what is happening in music.

The point of view taken here is that of discovery; the rules of traditional harmony are necessarily absent from any early discussions. This is the opposite point of view to that held in traditional methods of teaching harmony. But we know that the rules of any language can only be understood after a fluency in using the language has been established. When children acquire a language a need develops for precision and effective expression; when they feel the need to resolve a LEADING NOTE on to its tonic they are responding to a cultural pattern which has been assimilated. Had they not heard music in which this convention was observed, the need would not have been felt. Similarly, in dealing with the tonic-dominant relationship, they are responding to a culturally established idiom. But to present these conventions as the only means of organising harmonic sound effectively cannot be justified either on musical or educational grounds. What is relevant to musical functioning is an understanding of idiom and the consistency involved in creating style. Of course the rules of traditional harmony need to be discussed with children at a relevant time, in such a way that their place and importance is understood and their evolution clear. When these ideas are understood, it is also important for children to have experience of hearing and studying, and playing and singing music by composers who, for very good reasons, do not adhere to traditional rules. Children can then learn to judge the use of harmony, and are not employed in the sterile occupation of doing harmony exercises. But first they need to become fluent in using chords, and their progressions, and in arranging them between parts for voices or instruments. 'Mistakes' will occur, just as they do in children's paintings and poetry, but in fact they are not mistakes in the sense in which adults use the word, but reflect the ideas not yet fully assimilated by children. There can be no question of right and wrong while a genuine understanding of harmony is evolving.

Many children of 10 and 11 have not yet developed concepts of harmony; indeed, their harmonic perception may not have begun to develop. They will be at the stage when harmonies are produced in their work as a result of the pitch and organisation used. The development of harmonic understanding is dependent on the school experience children have, and this particular area of musical experience is one of which children are often deprived. The examples in this chapter indicate that concepts of harmony develop later than concepts of time, pitch and form. They also indicate a sequence in harmonic growth which begins with diatonic ideas and gradually encompasses twentieth-century ideas (see Examples 41, 70 and 71). Given appropriate experiences, harmonic concepts should have begun to develop in children at the top of the middle school.

SUMMARY

Concepts of harmony become established later than those of time, pitch and form. Harmonic sound is at first produced inadvertently as a result of children's actions on instruments; it is first conceived polyphonically as tunes are played simultaneously. The use of pedal notes, ostinato and ground bass emerges, in which no concern for precise intervals is felt, but as awareness of progression and resolution grows, ending notes and ending chords gradually assume importance and are considered vertically. Playing instruments on which chords are pre-selected is desirable in the early stages of harmonic growth, when children begin to harmonise familiar tunes. The small keyboard of melodicas facilitates chord building and the familiar sound of triads is soon discovered, understood generally at first and later analysed in detail. Experiments with other chord constructions are also made, for, given listening and singing experience of a wide variety of harmonic styles, children accept dissonance as part of the language of music, encompassing first diatonic and then more recent ideas. Only by becoming fluent in using harmonic vocabulary can children come to perceive the laws which govern style, and apply them to their own composition.

FURTHER READING

Addison, Richard   *Children Make Music*
   Holmes McDougall, 1967 (Chapter 22)

6 Writing and Reading Music

In the past, music teachers have thought that musical literacy is concerned with the ability to read and write music; the total emphasis in musical education has been on the importance of teaching children to read notation. This is parallel with the importance attached to the teaching of reading in infant schools: it was felt to be the basic tool for all later learning. However, we now consider that reading is not the basic tool, but one of the skills – a vitally necessary one in a society in which ideas are communicated verbally – which supports the growth of the basic skill of thinking. The only purpose in reading is the extraction of meaning: it is a means of furthering experience. Until words have meaning and a need is felt to use them as a source of information, there is little point in going through the mechanics of reading for its own sake. We have all met children who have learned their reader off by heart but who, in fact, do not actually read but apply their memory skill to the activity. There is a direct parallel with learning to read music. No value at all exists in reading through a score, however simple, if the ideas represented by notational symbols are not understood. There has to be a basic conceptual understanding which can be expressed verbally and communicated to other people, before an understanding can develop of representing the ideas with a series of symbols reflecting the logic of the system. Children learn to read music easily in an environment which fosters their understanding of the musical world around them, and reinforces their natural desire to find out about it and to learn to operate within its laws. The pressure to do so comes from within themselves, a need is felt and a course of action becomes necessary. This takes its natural course if pressure from adults is absent, and if 'reading performance' is not expected before understanding has begun to develop. To grasp that a sign represents an idea is a sophisticated notion. Symbolic representation seems to finalise the knowing of an idea and writing down a piece of music establishes it permanently, not only for the composer, but for anyone who cares to read it.

Our concern here is not with the teaching of notation to children, but with the development of their need to make a written record of their music. As we have seen, for the five and six year old a drawing of the instrument used represents the music played, reflecting children's absorption in the activity of causing sound (see Example 7). As concrete ideas develop, children begin to analyse the music they make up and their scores become a little more complicated; they may use numbers to signify the number of bangs, or indicate the patterning by the spacing between the numbers (see Example 10). Usually the music consists of a number of counted beats (see Chapter 2) with a space, on paper and in sound, before the next group of counted beats. These are usually played in time, the intervals between the groups being in time not intentionally but intuitively. After rather terse written statements about the number of hits or beats with a drawing of the instrument alongside, a rather fuller verbal description often follows.

I am going to do glissandos.

EXAMPLE 77   Girl (7)

| | | | | | | | | | | | | | | | | (| |
| | | | | | | | | | | | | | |)
floor | | | | | | | | |) |

EXAMPLE 78   Boy (7)

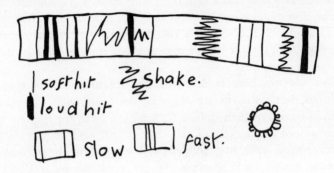

EXAMPLE 79   Boy (8) used a key to his signs.

Instead of writing the name of the instrument above their score, many children still find it necessary to draw it to make sure that there is no doubt about their intention! The use of drawings and numbers gradually gives way to the use of signs which reflect children's ideas of space and density; the symbols are often supported by a drawing or verbal description (see Example above). When children are using a sign with constant intention, and when the intention is carried out accurately, (it usually happens that a sign for a beat emerges as a constant factor as the concept of beat becomes established), this is the appropriate time to give the children the culturally accepted sign.

TEACHER 'This is the sign usually used for a beat.' (see Example 12)

To suggest that the beat *is* the crotchet is misleading and inaccurate, and makes for confusion when children later meet music in which the quaver, or DOTTED CROTCHET, or MINIM, is taken as the beat. When children begin to use accepted notational signs, they need help in analysing the components of the shape, so that the signs can be drawn accurately and legibly. Even in writing a crotchet there are pitfalls, and so help needs to be given in verbal description as well as in demonstration, drawing attention to the shape of the note and the vertical position of the stem (shown up and down).

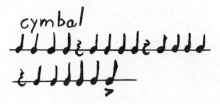

EXAMPLE 80 Girl (8)

At first no lines are necessary, as the first pieces of music which can be analysed by the composer, and therefore written down, are time patterns – even if they are played on a pitch instrument (see Chapter 2). Using plain paper at first gives children time to learn how to draw notes at the size they can manage, without having to accommodate to the difficult restriction of the lines of a stave. Children first analyse the tunes they make up by naming the notes; it takes time for them to become familiar with the names of notes and they need practice in talking about the notes they use in their tunes.

> TEACHER 'What note did your tune begin with?'
> GIRL (7) 'G.'
> TEACHER 'What note did it end with?'
> GIRL 'G.'
> TEACHER 'The same G or a different G?'
> GIRL 'The same one.'

EXAMPLE 81 Boy (8)

Wall charts of music made up by the children and notated by the teacher before the children themselves can do so, are of immense value here in giving children opportunities to become familiar with the look of notation. It does take time for teachers to produce these charts regularly, but it helps children to see the music they have made up written out; because they have made it up they have some understanding of it, and can therefore make some

D

sense of the score. There is also added interest for the rest of
the class in seeing the scores of music they remember from a
previous lesson. Example 82 is of a chart of work produced by
four seven year olds.

B.... on the cymbal

A.... on the xylophone

Notes F D B G E C

W.... on the xylophone

A pentatonic tune

D.... on the glockenspiel

He made a sequence

EXAMPLE 82

At an appropriate time attention can be drawn to an orchestral
score in which the percussion parts are written on one line, and
at the same time teachers can begin scoring rhythms on charts
in this way. It might seem logical for teachers to score time patterns on one line from the outset, but children need first to see the
shape of a note without there seeming to be a line through it.
This avoids later confusion over the use of LEDGER LINES.

Ordinary manuscript paper is of little use to children who are
beginning to notate their own music: a plain drawing book of

adequate size is necessary (30 cm × 20 cm). If they have a book, children can build a collection of their own music and refer to previous scores if necessary. Lines can be drawn with a ruler when they are needed, at the distance apart which children choose; those who find it difficult to draw notes on lines can then write in a large music hand (see Example 80). Using plain paper has another advantage in the early stages of writing music, for when scores are written for a pitch instrument with a rhythmic accompaniment, one five-line stave can be used with as many single lines as are needed for the rhythm parts.

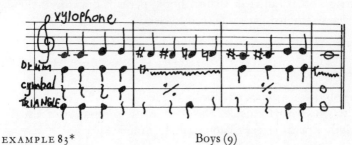

EXAMPLE 83*   Boys (9)

As the skill of drawing notes develops, they become smaller and neater, and the distance between the lines can be adjusted accordingly. When the skill has developed to this extent, manuscript books (not with the smallest size stave) can be used easily.

At first large Black Beauty pencils are much more useful than ordinary lead ones because their points are stronger and thicker and the pencils are a good size for children to hold. The writing is very black and can easily be read by children who have arranged their instruments in front of their books: it can also be seen across a room when books are put on display, whereas ordinary pencil is difficult to see from far away. Desk music stands are extremely useful at this time as they can be used on the floor or on any surface, according to the player's need. They are inexpensive to buy.

By looking through children's books their level of musical knowledge and understanding becomes apparent. What is written down in personal notation is obviously understood, as it had to be analysed to be written down at all. This is in marked contrast to the patterns of crotchets and quavers which appear in the books of children who have seen the signs and want to use them, but do not understand in any real sense what they represent. Of course, at times children play with notation as they do with everything else, and many a collection of notes is taken to teachers to be played to find out what it sounds like. This is a small part of the beginning of notational understanding.

When children are using the accepted sign for a crotchet they will soon need the signs for a crotchet rest and accent (see Example 21). A pattern of behaviour gradually emerges: the teacher is asked for a new sign when it is needed, and can show the child the sign on a wall chart or in a book, perhaps drawing it slowly as well so that its shape is perceived clearly.

GIRL (9) 'How do you write a three-beat rest?'

BOY (9) 'How do you write a chord? Do you put the notes on top of each other?'

The sign for a repeated idea is needed when children begin to write down their music, for their early compositions usually include repetition (see Chapter 4 and Example 83).

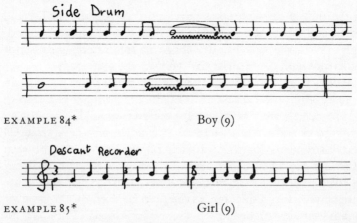

EXAMPLE 84*   Boy (9)

EXAMPLE 85*   Girl (9)

With the growth of operational thinking, when ideas become concrete and capable of analysis, there is also a period of social development. At this time children often choose to work together, but still spend time on their own if they need to work at a particular idea or problem; they also do this when they begin to write 'proper' notation for they have enough to cope with at first in writing their own music (see Examples 84 and 85). When group work is resumed, a FULL SCORE becomes necessary and a clear plan of the whole piece of music is written down by each member of the group. Children will be familiar with the look of full scores from seeing music on display which has been notated by their teacher; as they look at their group's music, and in particular at their own part, they are at the beginning of developing the skill of score-reading. To score music fully is a valuable experience in the early stages, though this can later give way to the writing of one full score and individual parts. There need to be discussions in class about full scoring, and especially about its vertical aspect which presents some difficulty at first. This is a spatial problem, that everything occurring on one beat should lie directly in a vertical line; it means that the spacing of whole beats must be carefully judged, if other parts have rhythmic divisions which need more space in which to be written down.

EXAMPLE 86*. Part of a score for descant recorders by three boys (9); this was their first full score. They were each concerned with reading their own line of music, and failed to see that a full score was not necessary as their parts were in unison.

Until the notion of the grouping of beats emerges, children write their music in an unbroken line and obviously find it easy to lose their place (see Example 80). As we have seen, the use of the accent sign often proves to be the linking factor with the idea of division into bars, and this of course will simplify the reading problem (see Chapter 2). When it becomes clear that accents are occurring in regular places and the grouping of beats is understood, organisation of beats into bars and the use of bar lines can be discussed, as well as the convention of signifying at the beginning of each bar the number of beats in it, if this is different from the previous bar: in Example 85 this had been partially understood. If TIME SIGNATURES are presented to children in the form of the number of beats over a crotchet sign (see Example 82), the idea of the top figure describing the number of beats and the underneath figure describing the length of beat becomes established, thus avoiding the lasting confusion many children experience when they meet 4 over 4 ($\frac{4}{4}$) and do not understand the significance of the two numerals. When it is clear that the significance of the top figure *is* fully understood – its use in writing and discussion is the only evidence – a full explanation of the bottom figure is necessary. Mention of the American and German system in which the names of notes describe their time value (♩ represents a quarter-note) is helpful; a reference chart is useful for this. It seems clear that there needs to be a time lag in the presentation of these two ideas, both of which include the use of numbers, but each with a different purpose mathematically. What is initially important is that children should learn to use the bar-grouping system and to signify any alteration in the grouping of beats. When they are learning to use time signatures, the placing of numbers on the stave needs demonstration and brief discussion.

In writing rhythms, first on plain paper and then on one line or on the stave, children become more and more skilful at shaping notes and in making the stems of equal length. When they come to use the five-line stave to write melodies, only one new aspect has to be taken into account, that of notes written in the spaces between the lines. If it is pointed out that notes written in the spaces on a stave are the same size as notes written on the lines, scores are avoided in which small full-stops sit in the middle of spaces and the notes on lines are of a completely different size. This particular skill of writing notation is not often considered in school in such a way that children can learn the rationale of the system. All these points of notation need to be discussed, either with the child concerned, or in a group discussion, or with the whole class if it becomes apparent that many children are coming across the same problem.

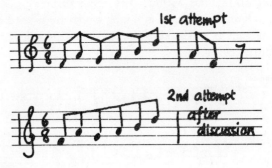

EXAMPLE 87*

GIRL (10) 'I've written down the beginning of my tune but it looks all wrong and I can't see why.'

When children need to write down divisions of the beat the movement of notes up and down the stave presents an initial problem; if they have become accustomed to seeing pairs of quavers globally as two notes joined together, they often assume that *all* groups of four are SEMI-QUAVERS, indeed this has a mathematical logic. Another difficulty is the convention of joining bars of quavers together, e.g. $\frac{3}{4}$ ♩♩♩♩♩♩. If the point is made clearly enough in discussions from the outset, that the number of lines joining the notes is the vital clue to their value, this difficulty should be avoided. It is helpful to show children who have grasped this idea, scores in which groups of five are joined with two lines ♩♩♩♩♩ (five in the time of four semi-quavers) or groups of three joined with one line ♩♩♩ (three in the time of two quavers). The irregular grouping of a triplet is one of the first to appear in children's compositions (see Example 4). Examples of analysis set by the teacher, of note values and the significance of their grouping, will foster children's understanding of the device.

The convention attached to the writing of key signatures can also cause confusion when, in fact, the logic of the system can easily be understood by children if it is presented to them at an appropriate time and with logical explanations. Just as the writing of time signatures follows the use of rhythmic notation, so the use of key signatures follows the use of accidentals in the writing of tunes. The convention of using all sharps or all flats to name the accidentals within a key needs to be discussed; at a later stage reference to music in which a mixture is used needs to be made, as well as to the significance of sharpened or flattened notes within a key.

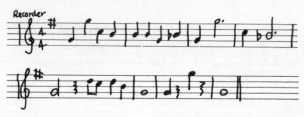

EXAMPLE 88*   Boy (9)

He was aware of the significance of B♭ in the key of G. He forgot to signify the change in grouping at bar 5.

When children begin to compose intentionally within a key, they need to find out about key signatures and the order in which the accidentals are written. Help is needed in placing accidentals correctly on the particular line or space involved, for very often the mere presence of a sharp, flat or natural sign in the vicinity of the note is thought to be adequate.

Many children have a very hazy idea of the significance of note stems which go up or down; some even think that this will alter the music. This needs to be discussed as soon as the stave is used so that the reasons can be comprehended. An explanation needs to be given of the visual balance achieved by altering stems above and below the middle line in melody writing, for this is likely to be needed much earlier than part-writing in CLOSE SCORE, for which a further explanation of writing stems will be necessary. A reference chart of two-part writing notated in both OPEN and close score can be of use here; in the open score both parts will follow the normal rules, but in close score the upper part will have upward stems and the lower part will have downward stems. Exceptions need to be considered as they are bound to arise in some of the scores children meet.

It must not be assumed that every piece of music that children compose needs to be scored: this would be far too much labour.

The more complicated the music becomes, and this is inevitable as children develop, the longer full scoring takes. To expect that every piece of music should be scored by children at the top of the middle school is unreasonable, the time taken from a probable maximum of two lessons a week is unwarranted, and would leave little time for children to learn new things about music.

A class of twelve year olds wrote full scores once or twice a term, though their manuscript books were used all the time for jotting down ideas and keeping a brief record of their work.

The learning of new notational symbols, traditional and modern, will continue if discovery and experiment continue alongside more formal activity in ensemble playing.

Full scores make an interesting display for younger children who are just beginning to write down their own music, and much of the older children's work will provide reference points for the work being done by the younger ones. When scores of the younger ones are put on display, older children often read them through to see what they are like. The simplest ones they can read with or without imagining the sound, depending on their stage of development. The level of abstract thinking which develops in ten, eleven and twelve year olds finally frees them from dependence on concrete experience. When this happens musical ideas which are *thoroughly* known do not have to be sounded either outwardly (with voice or instrument) or inwardly (in the mind's ear) to be read and understood, hence a further value of having on display scores by younger children, either notated by themselves or by the teacher. More difficult scores on display will need to be played or sounded inwardly to be understood.

READING MUSIC

The ability to read music grows from the ability to make a notational representation of it, whether children use their own signs or the 'correct' signs. The first actual reading occurs when children play to their class with their book on a stand in front of them, painstakingly, and often very slowly, playing what they have written. They probably know their music off by heart and would play it very much better if they did not use their book. But when a piece of music is scored for the first time, *this* becomes the present focus of attention. That the music is unlikely to capture the interest of the audience if it is haltingly played is not important; the peer group will enter into the challenging situation of someone reading their own music for the first time. When reading begins, it becomes necessary for the instrumental skill to develop also, so that the instrument has only to be looked at minimally, for the difficulty of playing a xylophone and at the same time reading from a score is considerable; this skill develops in nine and ten year olds as *they* feel the need.

As children's absorption in scoring grows, an interest in other people's writing grows. When a performance begins, children often gather round the player(s), watching the score intently to see if it is being read accurately. Changing books and reading other people's music – it is usually unnecessary for the teacher to suggest this – increases children's awareness of the need to give precise instructions as far as possible for tempo, mood, etc., if the player is to produce anything like the intention of the composer. This is the beginning of reading music. Following a score is an analytical process: it involves noting the details of notes and instructions, and forming judgements about expression. At first, the latter is an intuitive process, it is a skill which has to develop. To follow signals is not enough, for a rote response cannot make musical expression and results in a mechanical performance, however great the technical skill. Children develop an expressiveness in their stories and paintings in a manner which goes beyond their use of the actual materials: they need the same opportunities in music.

As we have seen, before children score their own music, teachers need to do it for them, and if this is to be of value to all the children, the score must be put on display. Groups of children visiting a music room will notice, read or work out, the music on display. Bookstands which slot into pegboard are ideal for displaying children's work books; such a display, renewed frequently, reflects the musical activity of a school and stimulates scoring and reading from scores.

The value of the performance (see Chapter 8) cannot be stressed strongly enough. As they listen to each other's music, children's perception gradually extends beyond themselves, and their own music, to their immediate environment. From a concern only with their own music, a concern for the music of the group develops and this gradually extends into a concern for music written by other people. The music written by their friends is likely to be in an idiom they understand well, but this is not necessarily so when they meet published music. When this happens, a whole new dimension is brought into children's activity. If a basic conceptual understanding of time, pitch and form is established, the new dimension is assimilated with ease. At this juncture, as large a range as possible of music written for the available instruments is needed. The music may be worked out thoroughly, or perhaps read through and changed for something else. The value lies not only in the reading of the music, but also in discussion of its idiom, of interesting points in it and of any notational signs new to the children; a critical appraisal should follow many of the performances. Much of the published material for primary school use is very poor indeed, dealing with the most trite of musical statements. Children realise this if they are beginning to understand music in any real way, and for this reason music must be chosen with care. Much of the music published for young children contains settings of songs, with parts for percussion and recorders, and in recent years the quality of these arrangements has improved as has the presentation and the material chosen. However, we have seen that children do not initially develop musical concepts through their vocal activity; their aural and vocal accuracy is dependent on their early action on instruments if they are to understand what they are doing (see Chapter 3). Added to which, songs and accompaniments form only a part of the world of music. There is a desperate need for worthwhile music to be written for small combinations of the instruments children use in schools.

At first the printed music available for children's use should be material which they can work out by themselves, and preferably short. Perhaps some help from the teacher will be needed, but if this is constantly so, the material is probably too difficult. When small groups of children work together, one of the group usually takes the lead and acts as conductor and organiser, but sometimes children wish to venture into the realms of printed music by themselves; this makes solo music very necessary. If children first meet printed music which they can comprehend, i.e. which includes musical ideas they have met often, the continuity of their work is maintained. On the other hand, too many new elements at one time cause confusion and prevent the assimilation of new ideas, and music which takes too long to work out will put off the growing interest in reading and dim the enthusiasm for working out. Children may choose music which is too long at first, and be unable to sustain the effort of working it out, but if they choose to give up, or stop at the end of a section, no harm is done to the music. As their skill grows they are able to sustain such effort for longer periods, and also learn to exercise better judgement in choosing music to play; the contribution of teachers in discussing their choice of work with children is invaluable. As children's understanding and skill grows, more complicated music must be available for them, for example, scores written for larger forces and employing more sophisticated ideas. If children have developed in the way described in this book, by the time they reach the top of the middle school they should be able to read a score in an ensemble conducted by the teacher, being subjected to the discipline of music and absorbed in its demands, and able to take suggestions and direction with understanding and musical co-operation. This may occur earlier or later according to children's experience and ability. But, at the same time, they still need to carry on with their own work of improvising and composing, for although children of this age behave with mature musicianship in ensemble work, they still request a time for their own work and experiment. The time-table difficulty ought not to be allowed to interfere with this need.

SUMMARY

The first written representation children make of their music is usually a drawing of the instrument(s) to be played, reflecting a present focus on action. As concrete ideas develop, numbers, spacing, verbal description and drawings are used. These are gradually replaced by signs, the constancy of which reflects the conservation of basic ideas. This is an appropriate time to begin showing children accepted symbols for the ideas they understand. Further signs are introduced as required, by reference to charts, scores and books, and by demonstration, for children need help in analysing the shape of symbols. A plain drawing book is necessary for scoring, not only in the early stages of drawings and individual signs, but also when accepted notation is used and rhythms written on one line. As pitch awareness develops, notes are recognised by name, and alphabetical notation is used; this is gradually replaced by the stave, lines drawn as needed; the use of manuscript books follows. Children's books reflect their level of musical knowledge and understanding. A display of scores contributes to pre-reading experience, provides reference points for the children's work, and stimulates scoring and sight reading. The examples in this book reflect the developing skill of scoring; most of them contain notational symbols used for the first time, amongst those already learned, and show clearly those aspects of scoring not yet fully understood by the composer.

Reading follows writing, as children play from their own scores, check the accuracy of a friend's performance, exchange books and read from music on display. The first published music provided should be short, employing ideas children understand so they can work the music out for themselves. At a later stage they are ready for more complex scores and directed ensemble activity.

7 Learning an Instrument

We have traced the development of time concepts and the gradual growth of interest in pitch, and have seen how the provision of tuned percussion aids this development. Alongside this new aspect of children's musical behaviour the idea of notation emerges. As their interest in pitch and its notation grows, children turn to the recorder for its specific method of producing notes in pitch; they are aware that it takes them a step nearer 'proper' instrumental playing. The provision of recorders is discussed in Chapter 9: they need to be available for children to use whenever they wish.

=sliding sound

EXAMPLE 89   Boy (6)

The sounds on the recorder were varied by the strength of blowing. His focus was on the rhythm and the intuitive balancing of phrases.

This behaviour is characteristic of a child's early experiments on recorders; fingers fly up and down in imitation of accepted methods of playing, but the focus is on the child's present mode of musical functioning, which at first is a concern for the rhythmic aspect of music. At this time little lasting interest is shown in learning how to play notes.

A girl (8) asked to be shown some notes on the descant recorder, and was given the fingering for G, A and B. She worked by herself playing these notes for three or four lessons. Subsequently the recorder was abandoned and she resumed her previous work as a member of a group. She declined an offer of more help from the teacher!

Four children from a group of eight and nine year olds asked to have some lessons on the recorder, and worked for some time to get the fingering right. They too resumed their previous work when their present interest in the recorder was exhausted.

This does not mean that these children would never be interested in the recorder, but that they were far too absorbed in the musical learning of the moment which did not yet extend to this instrument. A year later it was rare to find them in school without their recorders in their mouths!

A group of nine and ten year olds were all deeply involved in learning to read music (see Chapter 6) and there was a clamour for recorder instruction. Reference charts were put up for both F and C fingering, and the children devoted their work-time to recorder composition, and the necessary practice which this entailed.

EXAMPLE 90*   Boys (9)

EXAMPLE 91*   Girl (9)

Discussions arose about producing good tone on the instrument and perception of a tongued sound developed; the problem of controlling air flow was tackled for this presented great difficulty to some children. The instrument became the focus of attention at a time when everything else necessary for learning it, other than the specific technique of blowing and fingering, was in place. As a result the progress was rapid. By the end of a term some children were acquainted with the whole range of the instrument and were playing with skill and expressive quality. At the other pole there was nobody who could not play simple tunes, but it was clear that there were a few children for whom the blowing technique had little meaning. The demands made on the children by this activity were not so great that the focus on music-making could not be retained.

At such a time the presentation of recorder music is naturally of prime importance. We are fortunate to have available on record a wealth of recorder music from the periods of the instrument's popularity, and the simplicity of early pipe and drum music makes an immediate impact on children learning to play the recorder. In a class of ten year olds many compositions were produced in the style of medieval music which they had heard and understood.

The recorder music children hear, usually includes trills and MORDENTS and helps to extend their understanding of ornaments; as we have seen, the idea of decoration emerges earlier in their work with percussion instruments (see Examples 14 and 16). Many early recorder compositions include ornaments and children work hard to learn to play them well. New and alternative fingerings necessary in playing them, need to be given on request. It is often possible to give brief lessons to children who

EXAMPLE 92*   Boy (10)

are coping with the same problems, and on some occasions it may
be possible to talk to the whole class about a particular point,
but it will not often be possible – from the point of view of the
assimilatory potential of all the children – to give class instruction.
Periods of instruction need to be brief and followed by individual
practice and a continuation of the work in hand, whether it is
work for recorder, or instrumental ensemble, and whether it is
being read or composed.

Massed unison playing must be avoided at all costs, for if whole
classes of children play in unison they do not learn to hear
whether they are in tune or not: under such conditions it is
impossible to do so.

A beginner on the recorder, who had been a professional musician
for many years, was surprised at the difficulty he experienced when
playing in unison with two others. He could not hear and his intonation became faulty.

To play the recorder well, children must have the opportunity
not only to practise the skill of playing, but to hear the instrument in relation to other recorders (treble and tenor) and keyboard, in order to learn how to control its tuning. Learning to

play the recorder should develop aural perception as the children themselves are responsible for the intonation as. they blow, but the finer degree of aural perception demanded cannot develop if children are involved in mass unison playing. To learn to be in tune they must first hear their own instrument playing its own part by itself. The horror which strikes many adults when they know they are going to hear recorder playing is often not due to the nature of the instrument itself, but to the way in which the playing of it has been organised in schools. Music written for the instrument is not for massed playing but for various ensembles of recorders and other instruments; it is in small ensemble groups and as a solo instrument with keyboard accompaniment, that the recorder has its existence. It is regrettable that many beginners' books hold little genuine recorder music and usually contain collections of folk-songs instead; these are naturally meant to be sung and by their very nature cannot be concerned with the particular instrumental quality and expressiveness of the recorder.

As teachers, we should not merely give instruction about fingering, but should help children to understand finger-groupings. There are usually quite a few children in a class who have difficulty in learning how to use their fingers on a recorder. One reason for this is that they apply the principle of percussion technique, which they have learned, to the new instrument – and it does not work! The action of playing a recorder is totally different from the action of playing a percussion instrument: before a beater can hit a note it has to be free from playing the previous note. This causes many children to free all their fingers before trying to play a new note on the recorder, and for some of them, retaining the second finger on the top hole whilst covering the second hole with the third finger is very difficult at first. They need help in learning to think in terms of A and B fingering rather than thinking of an A hole and a B hole. Some recorder books begin by giving the fingering for G, A and B on the C recorder (C, D and E on the F recorder); this makes a helpful beginning for children as the successive taking off of fingers which is necessary to play these notes has a logic for them. Using these fingerings establishes the idea of finger-groupings in a straightforward way, and eases the transition to less logical finger-groupings (that is, from the child's point of view). Wall charts, with information about fingering presented as simply and clearly as possible, are useful here. Once children have assimilated the basic principle that groups of fingers produce different notes, there is no further problem in learning fingering.

If children begin to learn the recorder at a time when they have begun to write and read notes in pitch, one new factor only is involved in using a recorder book: that of following fingering instructions. Their understanding is fostered if, on first using a book, they recognise the finger patterns initially presented; their knowledge of finger-groupings can then be linked to the diagrammatic system used in the book. It is appropriate therefore, that books should be given to children when they have already made a relationship with the instrument and are using the first fingerings easily. Teachers do not always allow enough time for the assimilation of principle in education, being concerned that children should make quick progress. But if further material is presented to children before basic ideas are established, breakdowns in learning become frequent, as no core of understanding is present. If time is allowed for such assimilation, later learning falls into place with ease, and genuinely quick progress is then evident on many occasions.

The transition from percussion playing in which tone and technique have developed, to recorder playing, is an important one. Playing a recorder is possible for small fingers and small lungs, and at the same time the fingering, blowing and tonguing techniques bring the activity much nearer the playing of an orchestral wind instrument. As we have seen, early experience with percussion in a workshop situation develops practising skills: actually trying to hit a note sets this skill on its path. When operational thinking begins to develop, children want to produce exactly what they intend; when they are concerned with their own composition the standard of work is high, and there is no giving up until it is right. Because their first need to practise comes about in making their own music, a standard is developed by the time other people's music is tackled, and children know what to do. There is no question of stumbling through a piece more than once without stopping the next time to deal with the offending passage. Discussions after performances can foster this understanding so that when an instrument is learned later, concepts of practice are already established. Practice then becomes productive and never the meaningless, rote playing-through of music by children who have had no chance to build up ideas of diagnosing technical and expressive difficulties or of overcoming them. Indeed, children who have been taught to play an instrument without understanding what they are doing, often do not perceive what could be better in their playing for they have had no chance to develop a real standard. Lack of perception of a problem is not likely to lead to the solving of it, and if teachers are constantly in charge of operations children cannot develop perception of what they are doing, nor make judgements about it. A group of ten and eleven year olds asked if some of their homework time could be allotted to recorder practice; in fact most of them worked through the week, spurred on by the homework allowance. This also helped in establishing music as part of the school's work, making a statement about its importance, and took into consideration the sense of urgency which children feel as a new skill is developing, by giving it time-table support.

The first published recorder music which children use needs to be short, for obtaining satisfactory results quickly, fosters the growth of concentration and perseverance. There is little musical or educational value in most arrangements of folk-tunes for massed recorders and percussion. Children of nine, ten and eleven who are used to working in a genuinely creative way, are ahead of the musical understanding demanded in playing these arrangements, which are often beneath children's level musically and do not in any way tax their musical thinking and skills. This argument suggests that such arrangements might be of value to younger children, but this is not so if they are at a stage of development in which their *own* music is of prime importance. On the other hand, there is on the market some very interesting music intended for use in secondary schools, which children of ten, eleven and twelve are quite capable of understanding if they have been allowed to develop in the ways suggested in this book.

If children have worked in this way a sequence in their development emerges. The spontaneous creations of six year olds in which the action and the general product (i.e. music) are the focus, whether it is a drum, or xylophone or piano being played, develop from intuitive into intentional creations, in which simple but specific ideas are used and in which tone and technique are effortfully considered in the most familiar mode of causing sound, i.e. hitting. This usually takes place when children are seven or eight years old.

During the first period of the stage of concrete operations children's attention is still directed towards their own creations, as they gradually encompass ideas outside themselves from our culture, and learn to use and name them and to represent them notationally. They also begin to demand that instruments are played 'properly' both by themselves and by other people, and learn how to co-operate when receiving instruction. At first they are not interested in playing other people's music for their level of 'knowing' has not yet developed sufficiently for them to approach music outside themselves and make sense of it, but as their conceptual framework becomes established, it serves as the core of their knowing, to which new ideas can be assimilated, and which facilitates their accommodations to the demands of our musical culture.

The particular relevance of the recorder for nine and ten year olds is now seen more clearly, and its irrelevance for most six, seven and eight year olds, who can of course, be trained to blow the notes, learning the fingering by rote, but cannot bring musicianly understanding to the activity nor begin to be in any real sense recorder players.

The focus of attention of nine and ten year olds goes beyond their own creations: they are challenged to meet the external demands of the culture, testing their own capabilities in relation to playing an instrument and reading from a score, and using their compositions to work out new ideas they meet. Their compositions also include many ideas which are used intuitively alongside those used intentionally as a result of assimilations from the music they have heard. The ideas used intuitively give teachers an indication of the progress children are likely to make in the future; if they are intuitively used, and not too remote from children's understanding, it should not be long before they can be brought to children's conscious attention in discussion. At a later stage, at eleven or twelve, the subjective element in children's concern to meet the demands of the culture, gives way to a more objective approach with a concern for the way a piece of music should be played, or the appropriateness of the ideas used in compositions.

The relevance of learning an instrument at nine or ten also becomes clear: it is a natural progression which finally takes children into the adult culture of music. Ideally all middle schools should offer instrumental tuition on strings, guitar, wind, brass and piano to cater adequately for the sequence of children's development. As the purpose of learning an instrument is to make music, instrumental ensembles or a small orchestra (for *all* instrumental combinations) should be part of the musical activity of children at the top of the middle school, though all of them will still need time to work out ideas in their own compositions. For this reason it is also a *necessary* progression, for just as early instrumental experience of using percussion is necessary in the development of basic musical ideas, so learning an instrument is necessary for the development of more sophisticated ideas. However, provision must also be made for those children who don't wish to learn an instrument, so that they can take part in ensemble work using percussion, recorders and voices; their development will also continue, though ultimately – unless they become percussionists, recorder players or singers – their skill as performers will be less developed than the skill of those children who learn instruments, who will meet and solve many more problems of technique and interpretation.

This viewpoint is in direct conflict with that held by some musicians and accepted by many laymen, that instrumental tuition should begin at six or seven, or earlier, and necessarily involves much early rote training. But is it reasonable to suppose that the sequence of development of this area of children's activity should be totally different from the sequence in all other areas of development; furthermore, is it reasonable to accept without question this traditionally held view at a time when we are having to rethink our educational practices in the light of new knowledge of child development? Perhaps the heart of the problem is the traditional concept of instrumental tuition; the fact that we talk of piano lessons or violin lessons indicates the emphasis placed on learning how to play an instrument rather than learning how to play *music* on a particular instrument. Our concern ought to be to give children *music* lessons. It is significant that in several classes of nine and ten year olds, children who had had piano lessons from the age of six or seven lagged behind other children in their musical development. Their natural creativeness had been put off course by a premature encounter with the demands of the culture, and their musical thinking had become limited to the trite statements present in much piano music for beginners. They set low standards for themselves in their playing and were content just to go through the notes. While other children were becoming absorbed in the demands of scoring, these children had great difficulty in analysing their music in order to score it; when this was achieved the notation was often inaccurately written, for their global perception of the look of notation had not developed into an analytical perception. They were musically backward in comparison with other children. It is also significant that the exceptions were not children who showed talent in their other musical activity, but children of high general ability; children who pass more rapidly through the stages of development than most.

A teacher whose sole income is derived from giving piano lessons now refuses to teach children under eight, and prefers them to begin at eight and a half or nine, as she has found that children beginning later overtake those who began at six, both in technique and musical understanding, nor do they have their enthusiasm dimmed by the drudgery which is the fate of many six and seven year olds.

Another piano teacher keeps a stock of percussion instruments for the use of her younger pupils. They explore and experiment with them, and the keyboard, until their musical ideas are developed sufficiently to begin more formal work on the piano. She invites the co-operation of parents, explaining to them why this early experience is important to children.

In a group of intelligent and musically talented ten year olds the outstanding pianist in technique and interpretation was a boy who had begun piano lessons when he was eight and a half, the others having begun at six.

To place the learning of an instrument in the developmental sequence is not enough: our concern must also be directed towards the quality of music lessons children receive. Great care needs to be taken in the planning of peripatetic teaching, so that visiting teachers can be drawn into the learning experience of children and take part in staff discussions: for alas, we have to acknowledge that the manner in which instruments are taught by many instrumentalists militates against the development about which this discussion is concerned. Instrumental lessons should be an extension of the work children do in class, though naturally the study is likely to be more intense in the one-to-one relationship of teacher and pupil. Much discussion and experiment is necessary as new techniques are acquired and new musical ideas met. Children also need to continue their own composing using their instrument, for as we have seen, it is in this activity that they test out, and come to understand more fully, ideas they meet in music they are learning to play.

EXAMPLE 93   Girl (8)
Her concern was the movement in space of her hands.

EXAMPLE 94   Girl (9)

EXAMPLE 95*   Boy (9)

The fun was the putting together of major and minor chords.

BOY (9) 'You know the cadence of this piece' (perfect cadence in A major), 'well I've worked it out in different keys.'

EXAMPLE 96*   Girl (10)

As she played about at the keyboard she 'discovered' chords with
sevenths and produced a progression of them.

A boy (10) became irritated at the poor functioning of the fourth
finger of his left hand: his teacher suggested an exercise. As he had
felt the problem *himself* he became involved in attempts to solve it.
He began his next lesson by playing to his teacher several exercises
he had made up, as well as the one given to him. Over a period of
weeks his practice of exercises resulted in definite progress and he was
naturally pleased. Subsequently the playing of exercises, given or made
up, became a regular feature of his work when it was felt to be necessary, either by himself or by his teacher.

EXAMPLE 97*   Girl (11)

She composed this music at a time when she was absorbed in playing octaves.

A boy (11) learnt at his own suggestion the C major prelude from Book I of the Bach Forty-eight Preludes and Fugues. He worked very hard to become fluent in playing it, and then became involved in discussions with his teacher about its interpretation. For several lessons the focus of attention was phrasing, dynamics, intensity and timing. One lesson was spent analysing the harmonic structure. He began the following one by playing the first lines of the prelude in Db. The teacher asked him to play it in D, Eb, E and F and he managed to do so.

EXAMPLE 98   Girl (11)

Part of 'Variations on Pop goes the Weasel'.

EXAMPLE 99   Girl (12)
Her music reflects ideas assimilated from music she had heard; the
influences speak for themselves.

Children who are receiving instrumental tuition should be
encouraged to bring their instruments (if possible) to music
lessons in school. Their work of composing and playing in
ensembles needs to continue as before, but on their own instruments – if they wish (see Examples 41, 56, 57). Children learn to
be recreative on an instrument, i.e. to interpret music, if they
have had the opportunity to establish an understanding of basic
musical ideas in their own creations. Within any school society
children can become musicians as they can become painters
and writers, but not unless teachers organise class lessons and
instrumental lessons according to the needs of children as they
pass through the developmental sequence. This book is concerned
with the potential development in music of *all* children and the
majority of examples are the work of children who are not
especially talented in music.

However, those who are talented or very gifted musically do
not develop in a different way, they pass through the *same* stages
of development but more *quickly* than other children; an almost
instant assimilation of new ideas is evident in their work. The
needs of these children must be met as must those of slow-
learning children: both can make music.

SUMMARY

The sequence of children's instrumental development begins with percussion playing and the skill of banging. Learning to play the recorder is appropriate when basic conceptual ideas of time, form, tone and technique extend to include pitch, and when children begin to use notation and learn how to practice. This should develop instrumental technique and aural perception, given suitable classroom procedures in which the workshop situation is continued and in which massed unison playing is avoided. Music conceived for the recorder should be used. Having learned to play the recorder, children should have the opportunity of learning an orchestral instrument, piano or guitar; their instrumental lessons ought to be an extension of work in class and their instruments used for composing and improvising in general music lessons. All children need experience of ensemble and orchestral playing at this stage, although instrumentalists will develop further in musical understanding and interpretative and technical skill.

FURTHER READING

Grindea, Carola, and her pupils   *We Make Our Own Music*
  Kahn and Averill, 1972
Addison, Richard   *Children Make Music*
  Holmes McDougall, 1967 (Appendix B)
Franklin, Erik   *Music Education: Psychology and Method*
  Harrap, 1972 (p. 111)

8 Performance

In the previous chapters we have been concerned with the development of children's perception as they listen to each other's music. To call this a performance is helpful, though it is not in any adult sense a performance at first, but rather part of children's early learning about the communication between composer, player and audience. For children of seven, eight and nine the composer and player are usually one person; what happens in a performance helps the composer to make judgements about what is successful and what is not, about what interested an audience and what did not greatly absorb them, and about the music they themselves find the most satisfying.

Children's experience of listening to each other's music and of taking part in subsequent discussions fosters the growth of critical thinking. At first this is applied to the outside world, i.e. to *other* music.

GIRL (6) (listening to strumming on a banjo) 'I think that makes a different sound from the guitar; it's tighter isn't it?'

BOY (6) to partner 'We're not together.'
LISTENER 'He drowns the sound, D. does.'

TEACHER 'How did that music end?'
BOY (7) 'It died down.'
GIRL (7) 'It faded.'

BOY (7) 'At the end he did a loud one.'
BOY (7) 'I thought it was dull.'

GIRL (7) 'That was good. I thought it was like you playing.' (to teacher)

A girl (8) was so absorbed in her playing on a glockenspiel that she did not realise that the rest of the class was restless and fidgeting, because her music had gone on far too long to hold their attention.

A boy (9) lost the attention of the class in a similar way; he noticed that everybody was fidgeting but carried on playing, getting rather hot under the collar. He could not think of a way to finish other than by completing his idea.

As children's perception grows and conceptual ideas begin to develop, they think out their work much more carefully, trying not to include ideas which would be uninteresting. They are not always successful but have a tolerant audience who realise that music cannot always 'be right'. They also have a critical audience who are beginning to understand music.

BOY (8) 'It wasn't a tune.'
TEACHER 'Why did you say "it wasn't a tune"?'
BOY 'Cos it didn't sound like one.'
GIRL (8) 'It wasn't put together.'
BOY (8) 'It was too long for a tune.'
BOY 'Cos it got boring.'
TEACHER 'That's interesting: we have different opinions about that piece of music.'

BOY (8) 'She stumbled as she went up.'
BOY (8) 'It was a piece of sequences.'
BOY (8) 'It was lovely.'

GIRL (8) 'The 'cello was like slow thunder.'
GIRL (8) 'It was more like a haunted house.'

GIRL (9) 'It's an ALBERTI BASS in the treble!'

A girl (9) ended her tune on the fifth.
BOY (9) 'It stopped in mid-air.'

BOY (9) 'That was beautiful bowing.'

At a later stage children become very critical of their own work, setting themselves high standards in playing music.

BOY (10) 'I did that wrong; I played that note and I should have done that one, when he did a hard beat.'

GIRL (10) 'I made a mistake; I meant that to come down again.'

BOY (10) 'That was based on the triad; it was good tone, but it needed speeding up.'

GIRL (11) (after listening to 'Sheep may safely graze') 'It's lovely. It makes you feel beautiful inside.'

BOY (11) 'It makes you feel it's easy.'

BOY (11) 'Why is it that in nearly all music there is such repetition?'
BOY (11) 'It makes the point.'
GIRL (11) 'Well it helps . . . the audience.'

GIRL (11) 'If all goes well, we'll go back to A.' (ABA)
PARTNER (laughing, after they had broken down) 'We only did two bars!'

The skill of giving a performance begins in the playing through of music which follows a work-time, when the rest of the class are quiet and still, so that everyone can hear easily. A work-time is of little value without this, for it is only by playing their music to other people that children find out what they are trying to say musically, and how best to say it both in organisation and interpretation.

In many school communities children have opportunities to read their stories and poems in Assembly and have their paintings on display. This is a marvellous time for children to share their music with the whole school; if they are used to working out their music and playing to their class, playing to the whole school usually presents no problem. On such occasions the only new factors to be taken into account are the size of the audience and being in a conspicuous position! For such occasions rehearsals as such are obviously not necessary as there will already have been a successful performance to the class – otherwise the suggestion of playing in Assembly would not have been made by the teacher. But children naturally feel more at ease if they have played in the position required, which might be on a platform or in a (small) space on the floor in front of the rest of the school. For children's music to be played in Assembly is of value for *all* the children; the music of eight year olds is as interesting to a school community as the conducted ensemble of the oldest children. Even the simplest drum music can give great pleasure both to older children and to adults. In a school community this fosters the social relationship between children of different ages, for they all have much in common musically.

Three girls (7) played their music in Assembly (see Example 4). They each knew their own part very well and could concentrate on being in time with each other. Not all the children in their class wished to play in Assembly; not all of them *could* have done so, as many children were only on the brink of beginning to think operationally in a musical situation.

A trio of boys (9) arranged a recorder tune they had learnt with percussion accompaniment. They knew it off by heart but were deeply absorbed in reading notation and for them, no performance was complete without a score.

A group of girls (11) gave a performance of a CANTATA in Assembly conducted by their teacher. It was scored for first and second treble, descant and treble recorder, glockenspiel, xylophone, tambourine, cymbal and drum. Their skill of playing and singing and reading from a score were developed sufficiently for them to follow a conductor well.

In looking at the development of children's composition it is clear that musical expressiveness grows as basic understanding and skills are firmly established. It is only when this has taken place that creative energy can be available for musical communication. This in turn can only develop fully if children are experienced in communicating through the language of music: this is in itself a high-level skill needing both intention and intuition. Like all aspects of child development, this must be fostered in an appropriate manner lest it be put off course and perhaps permanently inhibited. We have seen that the idea of performance begins in the playing through of music at the end of a work-time, and this should be a weekly occurrence at least for all children. Playing in Assembly is a natural extension of this, for the situation is still a familiar one – the Assembly is part of the school day and is shared by the same people who gather together for a common purpose. However, a public performance is quite different. It is a gathering of people on a unique occasion in the term, or in the school year, for the purpose of listening to music. As in many schools a summer or Christmas concert is considered an essential part of the school year, the whole idea of working toward a public performance must be viewed in terms of children's needs as they develop, particularly as whole terms are often given over to the production of these concerts. The examples above help us to make judgements on this issue.

In any performance the music itself should be the focus of attention both for the players and the audience. Five and six year

E

olds may delight their 'viewers' with the spontaneity of their drum playing, but it is their action which delights and not their music as such. The criteria to be considered when making decisions about children's performances immediately present themselves. If the music is to be the focus of the occasion, children's stages of development will determine the choice of situation, i.e. playing to the class, or to the school, or on a public occasion, and the choice of music, i.e. children's own compositions, or children's own organised performances of music they have read, or conducted performances of instrumental and vocal works.

When children begin to make up their own music they need to play it to each other, indeed they demand to do so, long before they begin to use musical ideas when they are still concerned with their action. The main difficulty for teachers is one of time, for every member of a class needs 'a turn' at least once a week. Playing their own compositions in the class situation is a necessary part of children's musical development throughout the middle school, and should not cease once children are giving performances of written music. If this is a new experience for them, whether they are eight, nine, ten or eleven, it is likely to take a little time for them to be able to play in a school Assembly without detrimental effect to their music, even though most eight year olds manage this well. The same sequence of development occurs in children's first performances of printed music; their first hesitant attempts, with, perhaps, inaccurate timing, (see Chapter 6) are in no way presentable to a wider audience than their peer group. As an equilibrium emerges in dealing with this new dimension of interpreting other people's music, children of nine and ten are able to give performances in Assemblies without detrimental effect either to the music or to their capabilities. But these are still performances directed by the children themselves, they are not yet able to cope with technique and reading, and at the same time follow a conductor. This is a later development, emerging at ten, eleven or twelve, according to their experience. The skill of following a conductor without losing control of technique and reading is fostered if teachers first choose for this purpose music well within the children's capabilities, or something they have already worked out by themselves. Massive works, which might impress parents and visitors, are not appropriate to children's development when they are learning to follow a conductor in a musicianly manner. When an equilibrium develops in this activity, children are then ready to meet the demands of taking part in larger works: this is one of the long term goals of musical education and has its place at the top of the middle school.

How does this sequence of development relate to the giving of public performances by children? If, in the unfamiliar situation of a public gathering, children cannot retain their intellectual and emotional focus on the music itself, no real purpose is served either musically or educationally. Indeed if this occurred too frequently it would damage developing ideas about the performance of music, putting children in the position of acting at a low level of rote memory rather than being in control of their own functioning. Of course, a purpose is served if parents, teachers and children share an experience together, providing the doubtful element of display is absent. Surely school societies can arrange such events according to children's needs. The argument often brought forward that children enjoy such occasions is a spurious one, and is often used to justify what is inexcusable on educational grounds *and* on genuinely musical grounds.

We have seen how children learn gradually to view the world of music around them with perception and understanding. When they begin to look beyond themselves to music written by other people, an extra dimension is added to their functioning (see Chapter 6). Nine and ten year olds reach an equilibrium in their musical development; they are learning to read and to care about the accuracy and musicianship of their performances in the classroom, and are able to cope confidently with the demands of playing in Assemblies. This indicates an emerging ability to cope with the demands of a public performance without detrimental effect to the music, but it in no way justifies the spending of weeks and weeks in preparation for the event, which would be necessary for nine and ten year olds if they had to learn set pieces. The music which children are likely to communicate successfully in performance will at first be *their own*. Very little practice is then necessary other than to arrange places and continuity.

An end of term concert was given by children of nine to thirteen. The nines and tens for the most part played their own compositions with one or two recorder pieces. Items by the older children included compositions and ensembles some of which were conducted by the teacher.

Experience of playing their own compositions in public helps children to build up ideas about interpreting written music in public and to act recreatively in performances.

Singing will obviously be part of any school concert and practice will be necessary for this. It is reasonable to hope for a weekly time-tabled period for a school choir, giving an opportunity for children with a special interest in singing to work at an intense level. Singing practices should not interfere with the normal music work of children; if they are to develop musically their activity must be regular, and more than once a week if possible. Naturally enough the school community will expect rehearsal time to be taken out of music lessons, but if too much of the children's work-time is being lost, teachers need to use breaks and lunch-hours. One music teacher solved this problem by having rehearsals involving several classes of children immediately after Assembly when they were all gathered together! This is in no way to suggest that rehearsal time is not of value musically but in the early stages of musical development nothing is more important than the need of children to work at their *own* tasks. This is also true for ten and eleven year olds, though for them, given appropriate early experience, time taken out for a concert rehearsal does not interfere in the same way: their musical understanding is nearer the cultural discipline of music and they should be ready to function in a musicianly manner.

Teachers in middle schools need to take a very searching look at the whole question of music festivals. The writer recently heard of a school which had devoted all the music lessons in a term and a half to preparation for a festival: no other music had been happening during that time. Under those conditions it is doubtful whether even the singing continued to be a genuinely creative experience. This kind of preparation does not result in the raising of children's standards: what is true of children's learning is that points developed in one activity (on this occasion, singing one song) come to their real fruition in the learning of the next occasion (singing a new song). Continued repetition in fact defeats the aim and misses countless opportunities for development. However, children at the top of the middle school, eleven and twelve year olds, should have reached a stage in their musical development where they can cope with the demands of a festival in a creative way, without having to spend countless hours in preparation, that is if the teacher considers this a worthwhile activity.

From the point of view of children's musical development, it is clear that formal concerts are inappropriate for children other than those at the top of the middle school. But parents naturally wish to share in the activity of their children, and are helped to understand what is happening in school if they are invited to attend a music lesson. In one school parents of each class visited a lesson during the term and at the end of each term there was an informal concert of children's compositions, singing, solo-playing and ensemble work conducted by the teacher.

If musical education has as its long term goal the fostering of musicianly understanding and its attendant skills, we must put public performances in their true perspective as one of the culminating factors of children's musical development at eleven, twelve or thirteen years of age.

SUMMARY

The focus of any performance should be the music itself. If this cannot be retained, the performance is premature. First performances occur as children play their compositions to each other at the end of a work session, and begin to communicate through music and develop their critical faculties. As concrete ideas and instrumental skill develop, they are able to cope with the demands of playing to a larger, less familiar audience in Assemblies. Children can best learn to interpret other music through playing their own compositions. Later this extends to performances of published music, organised by the children themselves, and finally to performances conducted by the teacher. Children learn to co-operate in such ventures if the first works chosen are short and use ideas which they, for the most part, understand. More complex works follow. The same sequence of development applies to the giving of public performances, successful performances in Assemblies being one of the indications that children might cope with these without detrimental effect on their music or their capabilities. Rehearsal time should not interfere too much with general work in music and should be organised productively, avoiding constant repetition, which does not raise standards and prevents children from learning to contribute valuably when they rehearse.

FURTHER READING

Grindea, Carola, and her pupils *We Make Our Own Music*
Kahn and Averill, 1972

9 Music Workshop

If we take into account both the individual differences among children and the differences in their first school experiences discussed in the previous chapters, it becomes apparent that the likelihood of meeting a class of children who are all at the same stage of development when they enter the middle school is remote. On the other hand, we have seen that children of seven and eight are likely to be generally at the same stage of development, i.e. beginning to think operationally. So there can exist for teachers an expectation of the mode of mental functioning of eight year olds, and a diagnosis must be made as to whether this extends to their musical functioning or not. Before beginning to work with children, teachers need to find out about their stages of musical development just as they do about stages in mathematical or linguistic understanding. It is all too easy to be taken in by the sight of children playing percussion as they 'read' from a chart or 'follow' a conductor; for alas too often this is a mere rote activity which has very little to do with genuine musical understanding. Also, the fact that there may be a general level of singing in tune does not necessarily imply any musical understanding at all, indeed it is rare for singing to be taught in a way which fosters children's understanding of the ideas and skills involved. At present, school experience does not often allow for the growth of musical ideas: the skills and mechanics of music are still taught in exactly the same way as tables and spellings used to be. Thinking teachers however, have rejected these practices because they realise the utter futility of them before understanding has begun to develop.

At any first meeting between a teacher and a group of children it is important that an immediate working relationship be made;

it is a good idea for teachers to choose an activity which is familiar both to themselves and the children. Singing songs must surely provide immediate common ground from which the musical relationship of working together can be established. It is very unlikely that children will have passed through their first school without singing at all – even if it has only been hymns! This activity gives teachers an opportunity to assess children's stages of development of aural perception and pitch accuracy. Obviously, the initial choice of songs is very important as children's attitude to music in their new school is likely to be coloured by this experience; and as their concentration in a new and strange environment is likely to be difficult to sustain at first, short periods of time are preferable in the settling-in period. Students on teaching practice in junior schools have found that ten or fifteen minutes' singing time taken in the classroom each day proves most valuable in helping them to establish a working relationship with children in musical activity. In schools in which time-tabled periods are adhered to rigidly, the only possible course of action is to end the singing time when children's concentration begins to flag and to change the activity completely, perhaps to something which has nothing to do with music; for example if the children are in the hall an opportunity for movement work or some similar activity is created. To organise singing activity in children's first weeks in junior and middle schools in such a way that their needs – from the point of view of their musical development – are met, presents almost no practical problems to teachers who take music with their own class for, as we have seen in Chapter 3, a piano is not essential. If the walls dividing classrooms are not sound-proof at all, teachers can consult about possible times for singing, for example arranging it when the next-door class is time-tabled out of the room for P.E. or other activity. Although singing often proves a valuable starting-point in working with children, it may well be the last thing in which some twelve and thirteen year olds are interested. They may need something totally different from their previous experience of music lessons to re-awaken an interest in music (see page 145).

A host of practical problems seems to loom large when we

consider how to organise instrumental activity in such a way that children's needs are met. The first problem is the provision of the instruments themselves. Such provision is usually considered helpful and desirable in music teaching, though many schools quite happily manage without any instruments at all. But as we have seen, the use of instruments is necessary for the development of musical ideas and skills for we know that it is through children's own activity and manipulation of materials that they learn and that thinking develops as their actions are internalised. Their perceptual and conceptual development is dependent on their activity. It is considerably later that they can learn at second-hand without being involved in the action themselves, or deal abstractly with the problem in hand, without reference to the concrete. So, the provision of materials on which children can make music is therefore *essential* for their musical development. The great difficulty lies in the relative cost of instruments and the remnants of an attitude in schools which feels that music is a frill not deserving great expenditure. In considering the selection of instruments for children's use certain criteria must be borne in mind. The first is that initially children need to be presented with materials with which they can become skilful, just as babies are given toys and objects which they can manage to manipulate either because the necessary skill has been acquired, or because it is judged to be about to emerge. We have seen how banging becomes the first mode of causing instrumental sound, and how percussion instruments are appropriate for early experiments in making music as the skill of playing them can easily be developed. In the selection of percussion more searching judgement needs to be exercised than has hitherto been the case.

It is likely that some percussion is to be found in most primary schools, usually small and tinkly glockenspiels and triangles, and drums and tambourines of small diameter. These are easily transportable, easily stored and the least expensive to buy, but often lack resonance and have a limited pitch range. If pitch development is to be taken into account, tuned percussion must be provided alongside the untuned, and if an awareness of instrumental tone is to develop, and this is an essential part of musical understanding, instruments which are resonant and which have a good tone are necessary. This will usually mean larger and better quality drums, triangles, tambourines etc., and tuneable drums and tambours, if opportunities are to be given for the tuning of instruments. Larger drums will provide the necessary bass resonance. Very often the pitch instruments in schools are out of the singing range of the children who use them, demanding vocal accommodation to the octave or fifteenth. This is too sophisticated a task for children who are just developing pitch accuracy, and for this reason not only must the resonance and tone of the instruments selected be taken into account, but also the opportunities they afford for vocal accommodation: alto xylophones, melodicas etc. meet this requirement. If the instruments chosen have between them as wide a range of pitch as possible children can then experience more fully the relationship in aural space of notes sounding successively or simultaneously in melody or harmony. This is particularly necessary for the later growth of understanding of harmony and the relationship of parts to one another.

A second criterion is that children should be presented with the fullest possible range of ways of causing sound, i.e. hitting, sliding, blowing, scraping, plucking. As we have seen, the recorder is usually the child's first experience of a wind instrument and there should be sopraninos, descants and trebles in school, and if possible a tenor, though not many schools will be able to afford a bass. Providing a range of recorders ensures that children have an experience of parts in horizontal lines and the resulting harmonic effect. Wooden pipes, penny whistles and swanee whistles are useful as well as tuned bottles and hose-pipe of different lengths, and any wind instrument that can be acquired. Some schools have a supply of orchestral instruments; others will need to collect them gradually. Whether the teacher is a string player or not, and whether or not there are string classes in school, causing sound by bowing, and tuning and fingering strings is a necessary part of early musical experience. Any specialist teacher who is not a string player can, without too much difficulty, undertake a course of preliminary lessons and share the experience with children. Guitars, autoharps and chordal dulcimers give children opportunities to cause sound by plucking and strumming.

A third criterion is concerned with the inadvertent causing of harmonic sound. Obviously by hitting two or three notes at a time on a percussion instrument, a harmonic sound will result. Ideas of diatonic harmony develop from the use of chordal dulcimers, autoharps and piano-accordions on which chord progressions are obtained by pressing bars and buttons or by hitting groups of strings. Keyboard instruments are of course valuable in early experiments, and as there will probably only be one piano in a classroom or even in a school, there need to be several melodicas of different pitch. The haphazard putting-down of several fingers at once on a keyboard produces a harmonic result, most probably a dissonant one! Random blowing and sucking on a harmonica has a more consonant result.

A fourth criterion has already been discussed, that of the range of pitch and tone quality of the instruments selected. A wide selection of beaters, of different sizes and made of different materials, is of great value in the production of fine differences of tone. If the beaters are stored together in a large container, children have to choose the ones they wish to use, and this will involve them in making decisions and judgements about the tone required.

It now becomes clear that looking through a catalogue and choosing instruments which take the fancy and suit the school budget, is not a satisfactory method of equipping a school for musical activity. As we have seen, it is essential for all children in an infant, junior or middle school to have frequent opportunities to use instruments. The problem is how to arrange this to the best advantage. There are two ways of doing so: one is to provide in *each* classroom a small selection of instruments which satisfy the criteria discussed above, which can be used by a few children at one time. The other is to have a central, and perhaps mobile store, containing a large enough selection of instruments for whole classes of children to use at one time; a large trolley with three or four shelves and plenty of hooks and containers for beaters is ideal for this purpose. The latter is a better arrangement as it lends itself to a variety of organisations: it meets the needs of a visiting music specialist or of a class teacher who takes all the children for music. At times when music with a specialist is not time-tabled or in schools with no specialist, the trolley can be available for classes to use in turn, at least every other day, or a small selection of instruments can be borrowed by each class for a week or fortnight at a time.

The next problem which looms large is the cost. It is true that good instruments are not cheap, but it is false economy to buy poor quality ones even if they *are* less expensive, as their life is usually short and their resonance poor. It must be remembered that a central store caters for the needs of the *whole* school and the cost per head therefore is small; if this is assessed on a yearly basis it becomes very small indeed. Good instruments, even if they are used daily by children, have a life of at least five years and probably much longer, and only a small annual expenditure should be necessary to replace beaters, strings and skins which will be broken however carefully the instruments are treated. Most schools will probably wish to build up a stock of instruments gradually, supplementing their stock of purchased instruments with ones made in school by the children or the teachers. There are books which give clear instructions about the making of both very simple and more advanced instruments, and this is an obvious answer to a very limited budget. Another is to enlist the help of the parents, some of whom will have instruments at home which have not been used for years, and which they might be glad to give to the school; they might also keep a weather eye open for bargains in markets and junk shops, or help with the making of instruments. If the amount of money allocated for music is very small indeed, the selection of instruments needs to be made with especial care. The needs of children would be best met by buying an alto chromatic xylophone (one in two sections which can be used as one fully chromatic instrument or two separate instruments, one in C major and the other pentatonic) and a soprano or alto melodica, and making cymbals, drums, rattles, blocks, a set of tuned bottles and a zither-like instrument, and perhaps buying some toy instruments as well.

If all these criteria concerning the selection of instruments were taken into account and provision made for whole classes of children, it would not necessarily mean that musical development and creative music-making would follow. It is only by using these materials in their *own* way that children come to discover and gradually understand fully the laws which govern the making of music in our culture. In the past it has been felt that children should not be allowed to produce sound on an instrument in any other than the culturally accepted manner, and should therefore at the outset be told how to hold the instrument, how to use the beater, how to blow, or how to use the hands and fingers. This opinion was held, however misguidedly, for the best of reasons: that children should not fall into bad habits. We do not apply this principle to young children who are learning to feed themselves or who are learning to walk. The progressive accuracy of their action in relation to the end result is constantly in the adult's mind and each new step is noted with satisfaction. A four year old using a hammer will probably miss the nail at first, but will gradually become more accurate in his aim. This applies to any activity of young children. Adults note in their present function-ing the progress made, and see implicit in their action the progress likely to be made in the near future, making provision and presenting models accordingly. In other words children's activity is viewed developmentally and in progressive relation to the adult culture. What they do with lack of skill is not considered wrong, but is seen to reflect the stage of their development. This is exactly how we must view the first acquiring of skill in playing an instrument; through their own exploring and experimenting, children gradually become aware of the problems involved in a chosen task. At a certain stage in their development they will probably play a drum holding the beater very tightly and leaving it on the skin at the end of the movement, or play a triangle grasping one of its sides firmly in a clenched fist, or scrape a bow so hard across a string that squeaks and groans ensue. As their experience of hearing these instruments played by the teacher and by other children grows, the idea of making a good sound develops and becomes important; discussions on how to do it are likely to follow. In this way children are solving a problem which they have perceived and have worked to over-come. This is how they learn. If children have had adequate experience in first school they will arrive in middle school with established ideas about the skilful causing of sound on percussion instruments and the production of good tone. Eight and nine year olds who lack this experience and who are given opportunities to make it up, usually pass through the stage described above quite rapidly. Teachers have to respect children's present mode of functioning, acknowledging its appropriateness for them at that time. This may be extremely difficult for some specialists; if it is, it may be due to an over-emphasis on the discipline of music and a rigid interpretation of its laws, which they have allowed to take precedence over their concern for the development of the children they teach. If this is so, a decision is necessary which relates to the professional practice of teachers in which there is surely an obligation to keep abreast of new knowledge of child development, and to adapt classroom practice accordingly.

In recent years teachers have become familiar with pictures and film of junior children playing instruments and making music together. This is usually described as creative activity, but very often it is not. In most instances the children are acting under direction, either playing music written or arranged for schools, or improvising within a framework suggested by the teacher. The value of such activities can only be assessed in relation to the degree of understanding children have of the ideas they are using. If there is no understanding the activity will be a rote one, perpetuating intuitive functioning in children who should be long out of this stage of their development. An analogy with the development of language may be of value here. At the present time we are just beginning to understand that, until children are using language successfully in their everyday communication, until in fact there is a response to the function of language, reading has little meaning for them. Yet it is common practice to have children reading from charts and boards before there is any evidence to suggest that they are successfully communicating through the language of music. It takes time for vocabulary to expand and for syntax gradually to be assimilated, indeed it is some years after children begin to talk, that they are ready to deal with the written symbols which stand for the words they use. Clearly, experience of using the language of music and of becoming confident of its effectiveness and expressiveness will precede any understanding of notation (see Chapter 6). It also becomes clear that playing other people's music initially does not meet the needs of children if they are to develop musically (see Chapters 6, 8). Making music, improvising and composing, are essential in building the foundations of an understanding of music, activities in which the *children themselves* make the decisions. This is the heart of the matter. If teachers have any concern for children's needs at all, and if they acknowledge the value musical experience has for human beings, the problem of organising music work-times has to be overcome, however impossible this may seem at first.

The two factors which determine the organisation of a music work-time are the presence, or not, of a specialist teacher and the the supply of instruments. If music is time-tabled with a specialist it must be decided whether the specialist should visit each class in turn or whether one room should serve as a music room. It is obviously easier and more pleasant for a visiting teacher to oper-ate in one room, and as most schools have a room which is more cut off than the rest, perhaps at the end of a corridor, on a corner next to the cloakrooms, or in a hut in the playground, this is the obvious choice for a music room. A full-time member of staff who also works as a music specialist would have to use this room as a classroom, unless of course the school is lucky enough to have a spare room which can be used for music and drama and other activities needing space. If all the teachers in a school are responsible for the music in their own classes, it must be decided whether this should happen in their own rooms or in a room set aside as a music room. Such a room set aside for music work is very likely to have a dual purpose, making storage space and working space a real problem. The essential provision of instru-ments makes storage space necessary if the school decides that a trolley is not necessary. It is helpful for children who are learning to clear up efficiently, to have the shelves of cupboards labelled, each category of instrument having its allotted place. The top of cupboards can provide a working surface if not too high. Part of the display space of the room needs to be kept for music work and charts, and a working space on the floor is also necessary.

Desks and tables need to be arranged so that as large a space as possible is left, for when children are working at music, they need plenty of room to spread themselves and their instruments, particularly when they are in groups. Many children prefer to work on the floor with their instruments arranged round them, and if a large selection is chosen, probably the only place which will hold them all will be the floor!

If schools are adequately stocked with instruments, both purchased and home-made, it is possible for work sessions in music to be time-tabled for each class; this should happen at least twice a week if the experience is to be of real value to children. The problem is how to organise such a work session, for many teachers may feel that the noise and discipline problems are too great to overcome. However music lessons are organised they must inevitably be noisy: school societies have to accept this. But in organising a work session the noise problem is a particular one, because in one sense it is out of the control of the teacher. A work session should be a time when children are free to select an instrument, or more than one instrument, free to decide whether they work alone or with a friend or in a group, and free to choose their work, i.e. free to make up music as they wish. Teachers are in charge in so far as they indicate when the work-time should begin and end, and while the children are working they should be available to give help and advice where necessary, as the examples in the previous chapters have demonstrated.

One of the most efficient ways to organise the beginning of a work-time is to arrange the instruments on tables round the room, leaving a working space in the centre. Before children are told at their first work session that it is time for them to choose an instrument and play their own music, it is obviously advisable to have a discussion on the care needed in handling instruments and the ban on running or rushing in the music room. Some teachers might feel happier if they made it clear that children who abuse these considerations would not be able to use the instruments. But this should not be necessary: children's enthusiasm for using instruments is usually too great for them to put their work-time in jeopardy. Children of different ages, finding themselves in this situation for the first time, behave differently: five, six and seven year olds usually find an instrument quickly and begin playing it, whereas ten and eleven year olds with no experience of music-making may approach such activity tentatively and take longer to become involved. To provide the materials and the opportunity is usually enough to set children working, though some may need help in deciding on an idea. For some children the most satisfactory way to begin this activity is to organise some programme music or incidental music to a story.

A class of thirteen year olds began music making in this way; they chose to make up *Jungle Music, Traffic Music, An Accident, Foxhunt, A Train Journey.* The ideas were all their own and the teacher did not have to resort to commissioning music. They used a variety of objects to make the sound effects, including percussion instruments, and others, though not played in the conventional manner, and used their own signs for their scores. Their main focus, apart from the actual sounds, was the organisation of the music.

If twelve and thirteen year olds are retarded musically – through no fault of their own – the organisation of sound effects and pictures in sound, with or without a tape recorder, helps them to become involved in music-making; no skills are demanded which are beyond their capabilities, and the activity is sufficiently different from traditional classroom practice to break down any antagonism they may feel. Their musical development will begin with concepts of form and perhaps time and pattern, and also concepts of notation, contemporary not traditional.

When children are working at their own music, playing instruments and discussing, the noise is cacophonous. This is the element out of the control of teachers, who cannot organise children into making a pleasant sound if they give them this freedom to work. It is not usually a matter of decibels but of attitudes to music which cause some teachers distress in this situation. However, it must be taken into account that children are likely to begin playing instruments in a very boisterous manner if they have been deprived of the opportunity in their infant or first school, and it does take courage for a teacher or student to withstand the boisterousness of the first few lessons,

F

and to give children time to settle down to musical activity. But given this time to settle down, children become involved with the problems of music-making in the ways described in the previous chapters and the noise level becomes less disturbing and more under children's control. Most teachers have their own signal when they wish for children's attention: in a music work session a *very* clear signal is necessary.

A student on teaching-practice used a handbell for this signal; when she rang it silence and stillness was expected. She used it not only at the end of a work-time but also to stop everyone for a brief discussion of a problem that had arisen, and also to tell children if the noise level had got out of hand.

For whole classes of children to be working in this way is not the ideal arrangement, but it offers more opportunities for musical activity to more children than any other, until such time as practice cells, leading off a central music room, become part of all school buildings. Teachers and students who work in this way with children have few real discipline problems, indeed these are often prevented from happening because children are interested, excited and challenged by the opportunity to use instruments and make music, and are far too busy and involved to have time for any less acceptable activity!

It clearly is possible to organise music activity in this way for whole classes of children; without exception, students and teachers who have courageously begun music work sessions have been delighted at the interest and enthusiasm and above all the development of the children, though they all admitted to some trepidation on the first one or two occasions. In order to assess whether concepts of time and pitch have developed and whether ideas about form are beginning to emerge, teachers need to create such a workshop situation when they first meet children. Subsequent discussions throw light on the degree of intention present in the children's work, whether they made it all up as they went along, or whether they had definite ideas in mind. Their performance will also reveal their level of skill in playing the instruments they have chosen, whether it is a case of hit and miss or of highly accurate aim. It will reveal any understanding of the production of good tone, planning of endings and beginnings, louds and softs, repetition of ideas, of pulse, use of intervals, of phrasing, use of theme, etc. Getting to know children musically involves finding out where *they* are in their development: teachers then have to make the necessary adjustment so that their contribution from the point of view of the discipline of music is relevant to children's needs.

But if for various reasons a full workshop seems too difficult to organise at first, there are several ways of beginning children's music-making which do not demand so much of teachers or of school communities. One possibility is for teachers to choose five or six children to have a short work session in a break or lunch-hour immediately preceding a class music lesson, and then to ask the group to play to the rest of the class in the lesson; a discussion can of course follow this. When everybody in the class who wishes has had a chance to work like this, and therefore has some experience of both working out and performing their own music, a full workshop could follow in the lesson time. Another possibility is to choose two or three children to add their own percussion accompaniment to the chorus of a song learned by the class, for example a cowboy song or sea shanty. If the song has two or three verses, different groups of children could provide the chorus accompaniment. This could lead to improvised percussion interludes between the verses of a song without a chorus, and ultimately to a full workshop in which groups of children organise their own interludes or accompaniments for the performances of a song, and later work out their ideas without being tied to a song. Work in drama or movement might also serve as a starting point for music-making by a small group, and later by the whole class. As we have seen, the idea of programme music is a helpful one for those children who find music-making difficult at first. This is rare among children but does occur in ten, eleven and twelve year olds who are only too aware of their limited musical experience. Programme music forms a small part of our musical heritage and has its place in our musical culture, but to organise all children's music from the point of view of a programme, prevents their development in using musical ideas for their own sake, and exploring the language of music without being tied by the limitations of a narrative.

The use of a tape recorder often proves most valuable in focusing the attention of older children, who perhaps have made up music for the first time in their school life, on the successful parts of their work and on the parts which need attention. The recording is one step removed from their activity, and any initial embarrassment they may feel as they play is lost in the more objective situation of listening to a tape recording. Hearing their own music is of course, valuable at all stages of children's development. A tape recorder is really an essential piece of equipment in a music room, and in the present climate of electronic experiment it is appropriate for older children, perhaps in a music club, to experiment with recorded sound using simple tape techniques.

If there are not enough instruments for a whole class to use, children can be asked to bring a home-made instrument to music lessons; teachers need to ensure that they have turns in using manufactured ones. If it is genuinely found that the noise level of a full workshop is distressing, after it has been given a fair trial of at least a term, a workshop for half a class could be arranged. It might be possible for half a class to have music while the other half works in the library or in their own room. This should present no problem to children who are accustomed to organising their own work, but in schools in which the teachers do all the organising it might be necessary for the other half of the class to do some quiet work at the back of the music room. However, music classes will only be noisy for the duration of children's practice, for the lesson needs to include singing and discussion time, instrumental practice of children's own music, and performance and discussion time following this. In lessons of half an hour or forty minutes, it will not be possible for their work-time to last for more than ten to fifteen minutes, except on particular occasions, if the balance of activity is to be maintained.

The listening experience of children is also important: their musical development is dependent on their assimilation of musical ideas. It is appropriate to their development that they should become familiar with the sound of music from *all* periods of history, and music being written today; that they should hear music written for different forces, solo, ensemble or orchestra, and music written in different forms; that they should become familiar with the music of composers our society values highly; that pop and folk and jazz should not be ignored in school. Listening to music may stimulate research into the history of music and the lives of composers, and into following scores. Music needs to be available to listen to in schools as paintings are available to see; this may be as part of Assembly, or at lunch-time listening sessions, or as part of the workshop. Music may be chosen to satisfy the criteria outlined above or with a more specific purpose in mind, for example in a minor key or in a ternary form when these ideas are emerging in children's work. The personal preference of teachers ought not to interfere with the need of children to become widely acquainted with our musical heritage.

We are experiencing a complete change of thought about the role of teachers in the education of children. They are not considered any more to be the 'handers-out' of neatly parcelled knowledge, nor the testers of skills, nor disciplinarians controlling children's every action, but rather they are considered to be the creators of learning situations in which the development of children's thinking and skills and personal responsibility is fostered, and the needs of each child are met as they arise. This *does not* mean that teachers make no contribution at all and leave children to get on by themselves: it does not mean that because children's work is not organised by teachers, that it becomes disorganised. On the contrary, there has to be a constant analysis by teachers of each child's intellectual functioning and growth of skills with comments and suggestions and models presented accordingly; children's stages of musical development have to be seen in constant relation to the cultural discipline of music, as they grow towards the established ideas within it. Making opportunities for a work-time in which children produce their own music would achieve very little without the contribution of teachers, for there is obviously a limit – developmentally – to what children can achieve by themselves. It is the teacher who has to provide the necessary comment or suggestion in such a way that children become aware of the next problem in their work, not giving them solutions and answers, but putting them in the way of finding the solutions and answers for themselves, helping them to structure their musical experience and organise their own musical activity effectively. The rigid dividing lines between formal and informal, and between instruction and experiment do not apply to the learning situation described here, for as children develop, they learn how to work formally and how to learn from instruction, where previously they were intellectually incapable of doing so. Slow learners need the same experiences, but more of them, and take longer to develop musical ideas and skills. For some children the therapeutic aspect of music-making may predominate, either briefly or over a long period; for other children with difficulties, music may prove to be the first area in which abstract ideas begin to develop.

Syllabuses, programmes, projects, and graded schemes of work are superfluous: all that there is to be learned will emerge in children's activity, if their experience of listening, of discussing and of making music is rich. It is extraordinary that even in current literature which discusses child development in relation to music, the recommendation is that teachers should structure children's activity, and programmes of work are given. This reflects a basic lack of understanding of the central idea of child development, that children *can* learn to structure their own experience, and *need* to do so if their learning is to be of lasting value. Teachers who say, 'This creative activity is all right, but children have got to be taught some time', need to take a much deeper look, both at children's activity and the function of the teacher. At the heart of the matter is the kind of interaction between teacher and children described in this book, in which children's own work products provide the starting-point for all the learning and teaching which takes place.

When children have improvised or composed their own music, the task of teachers is to draw children's attention to what they have done, and to draw the group's attention to what each member has done, thus initiating a critical appraisal of the music, its strengths and weaknesses and the ideas used in it: to give the term for any new idea which emerges, not expecting it to be assimilated at once nor giving it only once, but repeatedly in the presence of the idea it represents: to draw children's attention to the way composers have used the ideas which are emerging in their work, and to play relevant works to them. Not only is the relationship of children's music to our musical culture in the teacher's mind, but the attention of the children is drawn to it also: they become intensely aware of their own development and are drawn very deeply into the world of music.

SUMMARY

When children of eight or nine enter middle school, they are likely to be at the same general stage of development. However, it is unlikely that this will be true of their stage of musical development, owing to the great differences in first school experience. Singing usually provides a valuable beginning in establishing a working relationship in music, and gives teachers an indication of levels of pitch accuracy and aural perception, but only children's own instrumental work gives any real indication of stages in all aspects of musical development. Moreover, it is essential to this development that a workshop situation is created, in which children are given genuine freedom to organise their work, bearing in mind that older children may need help to begin with. This experience lays the foundations of a genuine creativeness, and of the capacity to make musical judgements and receive instruction co-operatively. These things cannot develop if children operate within a format created by a teacher, or according to a set syllabus. The question is not of formal versus informal, but of the gradual development of formal thinking.

The instruments provided for children should have good tone, a wide pitch range, and should include all methods of producing sound. Whatever the situation regarding music specialists and music rooms, space is necessary for working, display and storage. Children should have at least two workshop sessions weekly which for part of the time will inevitably be noisy, but will also include performance and discussion and, at various times, singing and listening – aural work being an integral part of all the activities. Some teachers may find difficulty in accepting the sound of children's work before any real coherence becomes apparent in their music, but a fair trial of at least a term ought to be given to working in this way, either with full workshops or work with small groups leading to class sessions. This makes great demands on teachers, for a constant analysis of children's functioning is necessary in order to make relevant contributions to their development. This may be difficult at first, but the delight and·satisfaction children feel once they begin to express themselves through music, and find out that they can become better and better at doing so, helps teachers to relax into this way of working, and in turn *their* contribution becomes highly valued by children. The only remaining difficulty, which of course an enlightened time-tabling system could overcome, is the sighs and groans of frustration which greet the ringing of the bell, because *everybody* is *always* in the middle of something!

FURTHER READING

Music in Schools   Education Pamphlet Number 27
  H.M.S.O., 1969 (Chapter 2, pp. 12–16, Chapter 3, Chapter 4, pp. 31–6)
Dennis, Brian   *Experimental Music in Schools*
  O.U.P., 1970
Addison, Richard   *Children Make Music*
  Holmes McDougall, 1967 (Chapters 1 and 25)
Children and their Primary Schools
  H.M.S.O., 1966 (Paragraphs 686–96)

Suggested reading on child development

Flavell, J. H.   *The Developmental Psychology of Jean Piaget*
   Van Nostrand, 1963
Lovell, K.   *An Introduction to Human Development*
   Macmillan, 1968
Piaget, J.   *The Psychology of Intelligence*
   Routledge and Kegan Paul, 1950
Piaget, J.   *The Child's Conception of Number*
   Routledge and Kegan Paul, 1952
Piaget, J.   *The Origin of Intelligence in the Child*
   Routledge and Kegan Paul, 1953
Piaget, J.   *Play, Dreams and Imitation in Childhood*
   Routledge and Kegan Paul, 1962
Piaget, J.   *Six Psychological Studies*
   University of London Press, 1968
Thomson, R.   *The Psychology of Thinking*
   Penguin Books, 1959

Suggested reading on musical education

Addison, R.   *Children Make Music*
  Holmes MacDougall, 1967
Dennis, B.   *Experimental Music in Schools*
  O.U.P., 1970
Nye and Nye   *Music in the Elementary School*
  Prentice Hall, 1957
Paynter, J. and Aston. P.   *Sound and Silence*
  C.U.P., 1970
Schafer, R. Murray   *The Composer in the Classroom*
  B.M.I. Canada Ltd
Self, G.   *New Sounds in Class*
  Universal Edition, 1967

These books present many interesting and valuable ideas for musical activity. The ideas need to be viewed in relation to children's needs as they develop, and in particular, to the appropriateness of teacher directed or teacher commissioned activity.

Further reading

Blades, J. *Orchestral Percussion Technique*
    O.U.P., 1961
Blocksidge, K. M. *Making Musical Apparatus and Instruments*
    Nursery School Association
Cleland, Rees, Davis, Hann *Exploring Science in the Primary School*
    Collier-Macmillan, 1967
Donington, R. *The Instruments of Music*
    University Paperbacks, 1962
Holst, I. *An ABC of Music*
    O.U.P., 1963
Jeans, J. *Science and Music*
    C.U.P., 1937
Karolyi, O. *Introducing Music*
    Pelican, 1965
Roberts, R. *Musical Instruments Made to be Played*
    Dryad Press, 1965

Glossary

A⁷   The chord symbol in guitar notation for the dominant seventh chord built on A.

ABSOLUTE PITCH   also called PERFECT PITCH   The ability both to name any note on hearing it, and also to sing a required note, without reference to any other note. This is a function of pitch memory and can be learned.

ACCENT >   An accented note stands out from notes surrounding it because it differs in loudness or duration, or because it may be delayed or placed significantly in a melodic line.

ACCIACCATURA   See Ornaments.

ACCIDENTAL   The sign, single or double sharp or flat, or natural, used to indicate a departure from the key signature; the alteration of a note holds good for the remainder of the bar in which it appears, and only at the precise pitch at which it appears.

♯ sharp; raises (sharpens) a note by a semitone;
× double sharp; raises a note by a tone;
♭ flat; lowers (flattens) a note by a semitone;
♭♭ double flat; lowers a note by a tone;
♮ natural; cancels an accidental.

ALBERTI BASS   A very simple accompaniment figure made up of broken chords arranged in a characteristic pattern. The device is named after the Italian composer Domenico Alberti (c 1710–40) who used it frequently in his keyboard sonatas.

ARIA   An extended vocal composition with instrumental accompaniment found in oratorios, operas and cantatas. The DA CAPO aria was written in ternary form; Da Capo (D.C. 'from the beginning') is written at the end of the second section, indicating that the first section should be repeated.

ARPEGGIO   The playing of the notes of a chord in succession one after the other, instead of playing them simultaneously.

ATONALITY   The absence of tonality; as atonal music is not written in any key, there is no strong 'pull' towards a tonic (keynote).

AUGMENTATION   The lengthening of the time value of the notes of a melody or theme, usually by doubling. This occurs in Example 41 where the crotchet pattern of the oboe theme is played in minims by the clarinet.

BAR   If beats are grouped in fours, each bar in a piece of music is four beats long; if in fives, each bar is five beats long, and so on. Each bar is indicated by a vertical line, BAR LINE, drawn before the first beat of each group. The DOUBLE BAR LINE indicating the end of a piece, or section, of music is usually called a DOUBLE BAR.

BAR LINE   See above.

BEAT   See Pulse.

BINARY   Descriptive of music organised in two sections which are usually based on the same material and therefore not contrasting. Each has a definite cadence point. The first section begins in the tonic key and modulates to a related key (according to the closeness of the key signatures, see Circle of Fifths); the second section begins in the new key and returns to the tonic key.

BITONALITY   The use of two keys at the same time. This can be between a solo and accompaniment, between two different parts – including the right and left hand in keyboard music – or between two sections in an instrumental ensemble or orchestral piece. This is sometimes indicated by the use of two key signatures. The same is true of POLYTONALITY in which two or more keys may be used simultaneously, and perhaps indicated by several key signatures.

CADENCE   A point of rest at the end of a phrase or section of a piece of music, or at the very end where the coming to rest is felt more strongly. PERFECT CADENCE A harmonic ending point stated by the chord progression of dominant to tonic (V–I), commonly felt to express finality. See Examples 64, 72.

CANON   A piece of music in which a number of parts enter successively with exactly the same material, each part entering before the preceding one has finished, so that they overlap. The entries are not necessarily equidistant, nor at the same pitch; for example, in a canon at the fifth the second part enters a fifth higher than the first part. ROUND An *infinite* canon at the unison or octave in which a number of voices enter equidistantly one after the other with the same melody whose phrases are of equal length. The second phrase enters when the first voice begins the second phrase, and so on.

CANTATA   An extended vocal work, usually written for solo voices, chorus and instrumental accompaniment, though in earlier cantatas the chorus was frequently absent.

CHORD   Three or more notes sounded simultaneously.

CHROMATIC Literally, 'coloured'. Descriptive of music using notes other than those belonging to the key of the moment. Such music tends to modulate frequently. CHROMATIC INSTRUMENT An instrument which has all the 'black' and 'white' notes of its range. CHROMATIC SCALE See Scale.

CIRCLE OF FIFTHS A graphic representation of the relationship between keys. From C major the keys ascend in perfect fifths on the sharp side, each additional sharp being the leading note of its key. From C major the keys descend in perfect fifths on the flat side, each additional flat being the subdominant of its key. From A minor the keys ascend in perfect fifths on the sharp side, and descend in perfect fifths on the flat side.

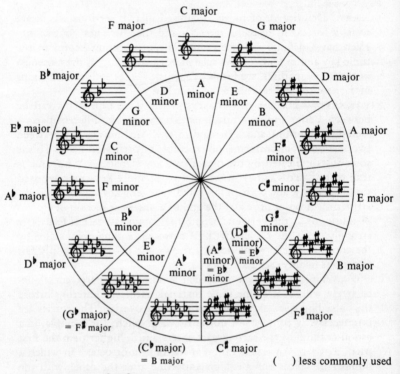

( ) less commonly used

CLOSE SCORE See Score.

CODA An additional passage, often an important one, at the end of a piece of music which serves to emphasise the conclusiveness of the ending. Such an addition to a section of a piece of music is usually called a CODETTA.

COMMON TIME Music in $\frac{4}{4}$ time is often said to be in common time.

COMPOUND TIME An organisation of time in which the beat is a compound one, i.e. has the value of a dotted note, and can be divided into thirds, sixths, etc. For example,

 two compound beats in a bar.

CONSONANCE The effect of an agreeable blending of sounds which does not need resolution.

CONTRAPUNTAL Descriptive of counterpoint; see Counterpoint.

CONTRARY MOTION The simultaneous movement of the pitch of two or more parts (vocal and/or instrumental) in opposite directions. In SIMILAR MOTION the parts move in the same direction (see the opening of Example 74); in PARALLEL MOTION the parts move in the same direction at the same distance apart (see Example 54).

COUNTERPOINT Literally 'note-against-note' music. The art of adding one or more melodies to an original one so that they fit together harmonically, but do not lose their individual melodic and rhythmic character.

CROSS RHYTHM Two or more rhythmic patterns played together, having a common pulse, but characterised by different numerical groupings of beats, or divisions of beats, whose accents do not consistently coincide. For example,

CROTCHET The English name given to a quarter-note, i.e. a quarter of a SEMIBREVE (whole note). It is very often taken as the unit of time in a bar. Its rest sign is .

DIATONIC Descriptive of music using the notes of a major or minor scale, or mode: non-chromatic.

DIMINUTION The shortening of the time value of the notes of a melody or theme, usually by halving. This occurs in Example 41 where the oboe crotchet theme is played in quavers by the descant recorder.

DISCORD A chord which is harmonically unstable and needs to be resolved on to another chord, either a concord or a weaker discord. The opposite of concord.

DISSONANCE The effect of sounds which produce tension and need resolution. The concept of dissonance is a changing one in harmonic style.

DOMINANT   The fifth degree of a major or minor scale.

DOMINANT SEVENTH V^7 The chord built of the dominant triad and the minor seventh above the dominant, traditionally felt to need resolution on to the tonic chord.

DOTTED CROTCHET   The English name given to a note whose value is equivalent to three quavers. See below.

DOTTED RHYTHM   A time pattern consisting of a pair of notes, one of which is prolonged by half its value (signified in notation by placing a dot *after* the note) and the other one correspondingly shortened; for example, a pair of crotchets become a dotted crotchet and a quaver   or   . Notes can be double dotted, the second dot further prolonging the note by half the value of the first dot; for example, a pair of crotchets become a double dotted crotchet and a semiquaver,   or   . See Example 67.

DYNAMICS   The term covering all the gradations of loudness and softness in music. Technically, these are caused by the degree of intensity of the vibration, AMPLITUDE, of a sound source.

   f   forte   loud; also ff, fff;   mf   moderately loud;
   p   piano   soft; also pp, ppp; mp   moderately soft;

$\diagdown$ crescendo   increasing in loudness
$\diagup$ diminuendo   decreasing in loudness

FIFTH   See Interval.

FIGURE   A musical motif repeated and/or developed in a composition; it can be as small as two notes.

v^7 See Dominant Seventh.

FOURTH   See Interval.

FULL SCORE   See Score.

GLISSANDO   A slide up or down the notes of an instrument.

GRACE NOTES   See Ornaments.

GROUND, GROUND BASS   A bass pattern or phrase or melody which is repeated throughout a piece of music (or section of a piece of music) over which varying parts move freely.

HARMONICS, OVERTONES   The pitch of a note is determined by its frequency. The frequency produces a FUNDAMENTAL note which is the basis of a series of notes – the HARMONIC SERIES – which sound simultaneously with it. These are not heard clearly because their intensity is less than that of the fundamental.

IMPROVISATION   Music spontaneously 'composed' on the spot by a soloist or ensemble.

INTERVAL   The distance in pitch between two notes, whether they are sounded successively or simultaneously. This is measured according to the position of the two notes in the diatonic scale. For example, the distance between the first and second notes is a SECOND, between the first and third a THIRD, and so on.

The SECOND, THIRD, SIXTH and SEVENTH are MAJOR intervals; if a major interval is increased by a semitone it becomes AUGMENTED; if it is lessened by a semitone it becomes a MINOR interval. If a minor interval is lessened by a semitone it becomes DIMINISHED

The UNISON, FOURTH, FIFTH and OCTAVE are PERFECT intervals; if a perfect interval is increased by a semitone it becomes augmented; if it is lessened by a semitone it becomes diminished.

Intervals larger than an octave are called COMPOUND intervals; for example, a NINTH is a compound second.

INTONATION   Good intonation means that music is sung or played in tune.

INVERSION   The treatment of a melody by inverting its intervals; those which originally descend, ascend, and vice versa. See also Triad for inversion of chords.

INVERTING   See above.

KEY   Music based on the scale of C major is said to be in the key of C; if it is based on the scale of C minor, it is in the key of C minor. Major and minor keys which share the same key signature are said to be related; for example, C major is the relative major of A minor, and A minor is the relative minor of C major (see Circle of Fifths).

KEY CHORD   See Tonic Chord.

KEY SIGNATURE   A sign placed at the beginning of each stave of a piece of music, between the clef and the time signature, which indicates the notes which are to be sharpened or flattened throughout, unless otherwise indicated. See Circle of Fifths.

LEADING NOTE   The note which is a semitone below the tonic, to which it has a strong tendency to rise.

LEDGER (LEGER) LINES Short lines added above or below the stave on which to write notes which are outside its compass.

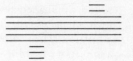

MAJOR (Latin – greater) See Interval, Scale, Triad.

MELODIC The melodic line of a piece of music is shaped by the balanced rise and fall of the succession of notes, and the rhythmic patterning used. The concept of melody is a changing one; for example, in twentieth century music much larger intervals are used than were once considered desirable.

METRIC Descriptive of playing or singing in which the divisions of time are judged with mechanical precision.

MINIM The English name given to a half-note, i.e. half the value of a semibreve (whole note), and the value of two crotchets. Its rest sign is

MINOR (Latin – smaller) See Interval, Scale, Triad.

MODAL Descriptive of music written in a mode(s). See below.

MODE A progression of notes corresponding to an octave of 'white' notes on a keyboard. Each mode has, therefore, a characteristic progression of tones and semitones; note the position of the semitones in the DORIAN, PHRYGIAN and LYDIAN modes.

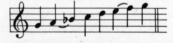

Dorian   Phrygian   Lydian

The pitch of a mode is not fixed and it can be transposed to begin on any note, for example, Dorian beginning on G.

These medieval scale progressions preceded our major and minor system which developed from the chromatic alteration of the existing modes – for example, the fourth note of the Lydian mode was flattened – and from the sixteenth century modes beginning on C (IONIAN) and A (AEOLIAN). In the last hundred years composers have shown renewed interest in the use of modes.

MODULATE To change from one key to another in a composition.

MORDENT See Ornaments.

OCTAVE   An interval of an eighth, for example C to C¹. See also Interval.

OPEN SCORE   See Score.

ORCHESTRATION   The art of scoring (writing out in full score the notes allotted to each part) a composition so that suitable musical material is given to the instruments of an orchestra or ensemble.

ORNAMENTS   The embellishments of a melody. GRACE NOTES   One or more notes inserted before a note of a melody or rhythm which ornament it, but do not interfere with the beat of the music. They are written much smaller than ordinary notes. ACCIACCATURA A very quickly played single grace note. MORDENT   An ornament in which a main note, the note either above or below it, and the main note again are played in quick succession. The sign for an UPPER MORDENT is ᜒ, and for a LOWER MORDENT ᜒ. ROLL *tr*〰〰 A very quickly played succession of notes on a drum in which beaters are used alternately. TRILL, SHAKE *tr*〰〰 An ornament in which a note and the note above it are played in quick alternation. In the Baroque era of music trills were played beginning on the upper note.

OSTINATO   A figure or phrase or melody which is repeated over and over again in a composition while other parts move freely round it. If it is in the bass it is called a BASSO OSTINATO; see Ground Bass.

PEDAL   A pedal note, or point, is a note which remains constant either because it is sustained or repeated, while parts move above it. The pedal note does not always fit the harmony of the parts above it, so producing dissonance at times during the passage. TONIC PEDAL A pedal note on the tonic (keynote).

PENTATONIC   See Scale.

PERFECT CADENCE   See Cadence.

PHRASE   A group of notes forming a musical unit; its shape is governed by the position of the climax in relation to the point of rest. See Example 52.

PHRASE STRUCTURE   Pertaining to the construction of a musical sentence which, however long or short, consists of one or more phrases – not necessarily of equal length. The balance of the whole sentence depends upon the elements of repetition and contrast within the phrases. Compare Example 37 with Example 72.

PITCH   The 'highness' or 'lowness' of a sound. Technically it is determined by the frequency of vibration of a sound source; the sound becomes higher as the number of vibrations per second increases.

POLYPHONIC   Descriptive of polyphony; see below.

POLYPHONY   Literally 'many-sounding'. Music in which two or more instrumental and/or vocal parts move simultaneously with an independent melodic character.

POLYTONALITY   See Bitonality.

PRIMARY TRIADS   The triads built on the first, fourth and fifth degrees of a major or minor scale, i.e. chords I, IV and V. Triads built on the remaining degrees of the scale are SECONDARY triads. See also Dominant Seventh, Triad.

PULSE   An equal division of time which, like the human pulse, is flexible and responds to states of tension and relaxation.

QUAVER   ♪ The English name given to an eighth-note, i.e. an eighth of a semibreve (whole note) and half the value of a crotchet. Its rest sign is ｱ.

RECITATIVE   Vocal music based on the natural rhythms and inflections of speech.

REST   A period of silence in music; each note symbol has a corresponding rest symbol. Rests can be dotted. See Crotchet, Minim, Quaver, Semibreve, Semiquaver.

   ▬   indicates a bar's rest, whatever the time signature.

RETROGRADE   Term used of music in which the notes are played in reverse order. See Serial.

RHAPSODIC   Descriptive of music in which the form and style are free, and in which the emotional content may be wide-ranging.

RHYTHMIC   Pertaining to the natural ebb and flow of the temporal aspect of music, as opposed to the metrical division of time. Often used to describe music in which certain notes or chords are accentuated to increase the vitality of the sound.

ROLL   See Ornaments.

RONDO   Extended ternary form in which the first section is repeated after each new section or EPISODE: A B A C A.

ROUND   See Canon.

SCALE   An ascending or descending progression of notes from a note to its octave, consisting mainly of tones and/or semitones. Scales which include larger intervals are called GAPPED scales; see Pentatonic scale.

MAJOR   The name of the scale in which the ascending proportions are tone, tone, semitone, tone, tone, tone, semitone; for example,

MINOR The name of the scale in which, according to the key signature, the third, sixth and seventh are a semitone lower than in the major scale. There are two varieties of the minor scale: in the HARMONIC version the seventh is sharpened, retaining the resolution of leading note to tonic: in the MELODIC version the sixth and seventh are sharpened when ascending, but obey the key signature when descending.

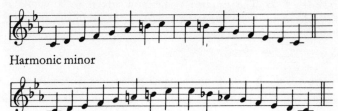

Harmonic minor

Melodic minor

CHROMATIC The name of the scale whose progression consists entirely of semitones; for example,

WHOLE TONE The name of the scale whose progression consists entirely of tones. There are only two sets of notes which form this progression; the accidentals can be notated either as sharps or flats, and the scale can begin on any note of the set; for example,

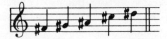

PENTATONIC The Greek name of the scale consisting of FIVE notes whose intervals are represented by the black notes on a keyboard:

It can be played beginning on any note, for example,

As it includes intervals larger than a tone, it is a gapped scale.

SCORE, FULL SCORE A full copy of *all* the parts in a piece of music. CLOSE SCORE, SHORT SCORE Instrumental and/or vocal music for a number of parts written in condensed form on fewer staves than in open score; see Example 76. OPEN SCORE Instrumental and/or vocal music for several parts in which each part is set out on a separate stave; see Example 41.

SECOND See Interval.

SEMIBREVE ◐ The English name now given to a whole note, though, as its name suggests, this was not originally the case. Its value is equivalent to four crotchets or two minims etc., and its rest sign is ▬.

SEMIQUAVER ♪ The English name given to a sixteenth-note, i.e. a sixteenth of a semibreve (whole note) and a quarter of the value of a crotchet. Its rest sign is ₇.

SEMITONE Half a tone. The smallest interval commonly used in Western music; it is the distance between adjacent notes on a keyboard, whether they are black or white. An octave is divided into twelve semitones. Smaller intervals, QUARTER TONES and MICROTONES, are characteristic of Eastern music and have more recently been used by Western composers.

SEQUENCE The repetition of a musical phrase or figure at different pitches, often on descending or ascending degrees of the scale.

SERIAL MUSIC, TWELVE NOTE MUSIC Descriptive of music based on a SERIES or NOTE ROW, i.e. twelve different notes comprising all the semitones within an octave which are treated with equal importance. These are used in a preselected order *throughout* the composition. There are various ways of treating the row: the series of notes can be used successively or in combination (making chords), in inversion, in retrograde or retrograde inversion; they can be divided among different instruments and not necessarily played within the octave in which they first occurred; they may be transposed and need not begin at the beginning. Not all serial music is based on a row of twelve notes; rows of fewer notes are sometimes used. Not only can pitch be treated serially, but also a preselected order of time values (durations) or dynamics or tempi can be used in a composition.

SEVENTH See Interval.

SIMPLE TIME An organisation of time in which the beat is divided into halves, quarters, etc., contrasting with compound time in which the beat is divided into thirds etc.; for example,

two simple beats in a bar   three simple beats in a bar.

STAVE, STAFF The horizontal set of five lines on which music is usually written.

SUBDOMINANT The fourth degree of the scale and one below the dominant.

SYMPHONY Literally 'sounding-together'. A large scale orchestral work usually written in four movements whose particular form was established during the eighteenth century. Previously, instrumental passages of music were sometimes called symphonies. During the nineteenth and twentieth centuries the form has been used more freely, for example in the number of movements, the inclusion of voices, or by being based on a programme (story or scene).

SYNCOPATION A transferring of the natural accent on to a weak beat, or on to a division of the beat; see Example 56.

TEMPO The speed of the beat in music. This may be varied during the course of a composition.

TERNARY Descriptive of music written in three sections, each with a definite cadence point. The third section is a repetition – though not always an exact one – of the first, which usually begins and ends in the tonic key. Contrasting material in a new key(s) is usually found in the middle section. A B A, or A¹ B A².

TETRACHORD The Greek name given to the FOUR notes whose compass is a perfect fourth and whose progression consists of two tones and a semitone in various orders. Two tetrachords consisting of the fixed progression of tone, tone, semitone, form a major scale.

TIED NOTES Adjacent notes of the same pitch whose values are added together, so prolonging the first note by the duration of the note(s) to which it is tied. This is indicated by curved lines between the notes involved, and can occur across a bar line. See Examples 54, 64; for example,

THIRD See Interval.

TIME PATTERN A group of notes of differing duration. The group may consist entirely of notes whose values are different, for example, ♩♫♫ , or one or more of the notes may be repeated, for example, ♩♫♩♩ , or a small group may be repeated within the pattern, for example, ♩♫♩♫ .

TIME SIGNATURE   A sign placed at the beginning of a piece of music, after the key signature, which in SIMPLE time indicates the number of beats in a bar (top figure) and the value of each beat (bottom figure); for example, $\frac{5}{4}$ means five crotchet beats in a bar. In COMPOUND time, the top figure indicates the number of units of time in a bar, and the value of each unit is indicated by the bottom figure; for example, $\frac{6}{8}$ means six quavers in a bar, or *two* compound beats. See Compound Time.

TONALITY   The use of one key at a time, in which there is a strong 'pull' towards the tonic. See also Atonality, Bitonality.

TONE   The interval consisting of two semitones, for example C to D, or E to F♯. See also Interval.

TONE, TONE COLOUR, TIMBRE   The quality of a musical sound which can be described as harsh, full, thin, warm etc. This is dependent on the number and relative strengths of the HARMONICS present.

TONIC, KEYNOTE   The first degree of a major or minor scale. The names of the degrees of the scale are: first – TONIC, second – SUPER-TONIC, third – MEDIANT, fourth – SUBDOMINANT, fifth – DOMINANT, sixth – SUBMEDIANT, seventh – LEADING NOTE.

TONIC CHORD, KEYCHORD, CHORD I   The triad whose root is the tonic note. Triads can be built on each degree of the scale; see Primary Triads, Triad.

TONIC PEDAL   See Pedal.

TRANSPOSITION   The act of writing or playing music at a different pitch from the original.

TRIAD   A chord consisting of a note (the root) and the third and fifth above it. If the root is the bass note of the chord, it is in ROOT POSITION; if the third is the bass note, it is in FIRST INVERSION; if the fifth is the bass note, it is in SECOND INVERSION.

A MAJOR TRIAD (a) is built of a root and the major third and perfect fifth above it; a MINOR TRIAD (b) is built of a root and the minor third and perfect fifth above it; a DIMINISHED TRIAD (c) is built of a root and the minor third and diminished fifth above it; an AUGMENTED TRIAD (d) is built of a root and the major third and augmented fifth above it.

TRILL   See Ornaments.

TRIPLET   A group of three equal notes, or notes and rests, replacing a group of two, four or more notes (in even numbers) of the

same time value. For example, written ♪♪♪ when replacing ♪♪, or
♩♩♩ when replacing ♩♩♩♩ .

UNISON   The simultaneous singing or playing of the same note by
more than one voice or instrument.

WHOLE TONE SCALE   See Scale.

Index

ten and eleven year olds
  compositions of, 50-1
  and problems of composer, 49
  use of formulae, 44
ternary form, 69-70, 74-6
tetrachord, 44
theme, children's list of developments
  for, 67-8
thirds, 38-40
tied notes, 32
time
  concepts of, 145-6
  keeping in, 23
  simple and compound, 29
time patterns, 13, 27, 30, 55, 97-8
  concrete ideas of, 22
  used intuitively, 15-17, 26
time signatures, 102
tonality, 40, 45, 49
tone
  concept of, 14, 18
  production of (good), 35, 137-8
tonic, 41, 89
transposition, 46-8
triads, primary, 89
triangles, 26, 137-8
trolley (for instruments), 139-40, 143
tuned bottles, 138, 140
tunes
  first experiences with, 17, 37
  for sight-singing, 56
  singing of, 53

twelve year olds
  history of scales by, 46
  with no interest in music, 136
  and music festivals, 133
  musically retarded, 145
  produce book on scales, 46

unaccompanied singing, necessity for,
  55
unison playing, 113-14

vibration, experiments and effects, 27
visiting teachers, 120, 140, 142-3
vocal range, 47, 52-5
voice, breaking of, 52

whistles and pipes, 138
whole tone scale, 49
work-time (sessions)
  to organise, 143-6
  problem of noise, 145-6
  sequel to, 128
  small group, ideas for, 147
writing activity, 9
writing of music, 94-105
  equipment for, 98-9
  group work in, 101

xylophone, 15, 29, 35-6, 40, 82, 106, 117,
  138
  chromatic, 42, 140

zithers, 27